Martyrs of our Time

Martyrs of our Time

by

WILLIAM PURCELL

Canon Emeritus of Worcester Cathedral

All these persons died in faith. They were not yet in possession of the things promised, but had seen them far ahead and hailed them, and confessed themselves no more than strangers or passing travellers on earth. Those who use such language show plainly that they are looking for a country of their own. If their hearts had been in the country they had left, they could have found opportunity to return. Instead, we find them longing for a better country – I mean, the heavenly one. That is why God is not ashamed to be called their God; he has a city ready for them.

Heb. 11. 13–16.

CBP Press
St. Louis, Missouri

First published 1983
by A. R. Mowbray & Co. Ltd
Saint Thomas House, Becket Street,
Oxford, OX1 1SJ

Library of Congress Cataloging in Publication Data

Purcell, William.
   Martyrs of our time.

   Reprint. Originally published: London : Mowbray, 1983.
   Bibliography: p.
   1. Christian martyrs—Biography. I. Title.
BR1608.5.P87   1985   272′.9′0922 [B]   85-4104
ISBN 0-8272-2317-X

Printed in the United States of America

FOREWORD

The people of faith so vividly catalogued by the writer to the Hebrews, those passing travellers on earth, longing for a better country, constitute a great cloud of witnesses, no mere spectators, but people who encourage us by the manner in which they stand up in faith, obedience and suffering, and refuse to compromise. We need their tough courage for we are called to be Christians in a century of martyrs.

William Purcell presents us with another distinguished roll of honour, covering the last sixty years. The backgrounds of these men and women and the circumstances leading to their martyrdom have been examined. Do we ever learn from history? Could it be that for most of us the challenge of witnessing to our faith through the way we live our life is to determine at what point we intervene in the inexorable march of circumstances and so help to ensure that Auschwitz and Hiroshima and the hounding of blacks at Selma are not inevitable? If Martin Luther King is right, 'man is not a helpless drifter in the river of existence, but an active agent in the unfolding events by which he is surrounded'. In the ordinary traffic of everyday life, most of us cannot transcend our differences – race, colour, religion, beliefs, class, age, family. We cannot let go of our treasured idols sufficiently to allow the tide of Christ's love which is in us to carry us on to new shores. In a world alienated from God, but not abandoned by Him, the only common language is that of love, the agape which can reach out to the unlovable and repulsive. Here is the paradox of Jesus inviting sinners, not virtuous people, coming to meet us at the bottom of our stairways, not at the top.

The scope of this book reveals that martyrdom wears many faces. The challenge of faith comes to each of us today in a unique way, because of our differing circumstances and personalities. How obsessively it appears that God is occupied with folly and weakness. Each of us is a microcosm of a confused and mixed-up universe. Perhaps I have to acknowledge that I share more in the sin of the persecutor than in the glory of the martyrdom for I am involved in *all* mankind.

And so the throng of witnesses around us, the martyrs of all ages, challenge us to rid ourselves of lumber, all those ecclesiastical antimacassars. Our faith is in Jesus, the one who brings good news and proclaims liberty and release, and calls us to embrace the faith which is God's gift, and which makes us certain of realities we do not see. The future is full of danger and anxiety. We can find temporary safety in clinging to the current idol of the heart, but our true nature cannot allow us to be content with this. Are we ready to leave the familiar cities of Mesopotamia for the freshness and openness of a tent-dwelling existence – to be a pilgrim people? God is always calling us on to a future where we shall find to our surprise that He is with us at the end of the journey, just as He was at the beginning. We are grateful to the author for reminding us of these heroic men and women who find the peace of God in not allowing themselves to be destroyed by the seductions of an easy-going deeply compromised way of life.

It is no accident that an increasing number of cathedrals commemorate modern martyrs – Canterbury, St Paul's, St Alban's, Salisbury and Norwich and many more. Now William Purcell has given us a well researched record. May this fine volume find a permanent place in the worship and teaching of the Church.

1983   ALAN WEBSTER
                                         Dean of St Paul's

PREFACE

All the martyrdoms described in this book took place in the twentieth century. All but two happened during or since the Second World War. Seven, including those of Archbishops Luwum in Uganda, Romero in Salvador, Steve Biko in South Africa, and thirteen members of the Elim Pentecostal Church – nine adults and four children – in what is now Zimbabwe, were events sufficiently recent as to feature in news bulletins of the day. This must therefore be the first age in which martyrdoms have appeared from time to time as news stories. Such a grim fact, however, makes the documentation of them easier than it might have been in times past. Several have formed the subjects of books. Such as have been consulted, are listed at the end of this volume, and their help is warmly acknowledged. So also is that of various individuals including the Dean of St Pauls, for permission to examine the Book of Martyrs in that cathedral; to the Dean of Canterbury, for information regarding the similar list kept there; to Mr David Ayling of The Elim Pentecostal Church, and to Charles W. Eagles, Vanderbilt University, Tennessee. Acknowledgements are also made to Hodder & Stoughton Ltd for permission to quote from *The Rainbow and the Thunder* by Phyllis Thompson, and *The Life and Death of Dietrich Bonhoeffer* by Mary Bosanquet; to Marshall, Morgan and Scott Ltd for permission to quote from *Janani* by Margaret Ford; to Lutterworth Press for permission to quote from *Archbishop Romero* by Placido Erdozain; to Penguin Books Ltd for permission to quote from *Righteous Gentile* by John Bierman. To Harper and Row, Publishers, Inc, for permission to quote from *The Martyrs*, by Jack Mendelsohn, and to Curtis Brown Group Ltd for permission to quote from *The Desert My Dwelling Place*, by Elizabeth Hamilton 1968.

W.E.P.

MARTYRS OF OUR TIME

Charles de Foucauld	1916
John and Betty Stam	1934
Maximilian Kolbe	1941
Edith Stein	1942
Alfred Sadd and Vivian Redlich	1942
Leonard Wilson	1942
Raoul Wallenburg	1944
Dietrich Bonhoeffer	1945
Andrew Kaguru	1953
Jonathan Daniels	1965
Martin Luther King	1968
Janani Luwum	1977
Steve Biko	1977
Thirteen members of the Elim Pentecostal Church	1978
Oscar Romero	1980

CONTENTS

INTRODUCTION

St Pauls Cathedral has a Book of Martyrs, kept in a glass case in a side chapel. There are many names recorded in it, and before they can be examined a verger unlocks the case, puts on white gloves, and reverently turns the pages. Canterbury Cathedral has the Chapel of Saints and Martyrs of Our Own Times. There, at a service on 29 May 1982, on the occasion of the visit of Pope John Paul II, seven representative Church figures placed a lighted candle in a seven-branched holder on the altar, in an action, as was said at the time, 'symbolizing our common hope and vision for the future'.

They were commemorating on that occasion the unknown martyrs of our time. But many are known, as the lists kept in St Pauls and Canterbury bear witness. The stories of some of them feature in this book. There are also others who do not, and the reasons why these are included, such as Raoul Wallenburg the Swedish diplomat, will be made plain.

There is a mystery posed by the lives of martyrs, those heroic figures on the Christian scene who seem to have been prepared, in many cases, to prefer to die rather than to betray their beliefs. What motivates them? What exactly was it which made Edith Stein, heroically to face an end in Auschwitz Concentration Camp rather than to conceal her identity beforehand, sufficient to evade that fate? What motivated Janani Luwum to face up to Idi Amin in Uganda? What compelled Archbishop Romero, by nature a timid man, so to risk his life in championing the oppressed poor in Salvador, that eventually his life was taken from him, by a bullet through the heart when he was saying Mass?

One thing is plain: martyrs do not belong, as is often supposed, only to the past. They are to be found in the present. The Church calendar, with its scattering of names from distant times, such as Agnes, Virgin and Martyr, AD 304, Justin, Martyr at Rome in 165, gives an impression

1

of antiquity, as though such persons may have lived then; but not now. But they do live now, and their stories appear from time to time in the news of the day. It is not long, for example, since the report came through of the violent deaths of a number of Churches of Christ missionaries in Zimbabwe, whose deaths arose from their faith.

As is stated in Canterbury's chapel: '. . . already in the 1930s it was clear that our own century was becoming a century of Christian martyrdom without parallel since the early centuries of the Church. Since then this fact has become steadily more evident. Men and women from all the traditions of Christendom have given their lives for the faith of Christ, under many different tyrannies and in fact of many different oppressions. If the Church has been given any true renewal of life and unity in our times, surely the deaths of those who have given their lives in union with the life-giving death of our one Lord Jesus Christ, have played a great part in this recovery of inner strength and vision. Here in Canterbury we mean to thank God for his mercies of blood, for all the signs which he gives us through his martyrs and saints, that he is with us, and that now, no less than in former times, the power of Christ revealed in suffering love, can overcome all that separates us from one another and from him.'

But there is another point which needs to be clear. Not all martyrs necessarily suffer death in order to qualify for the title. That is why there has always been a distinction between 'red' (in the sense of bloody) martyrs, who have indeed died for the faith, and 'white' martyrs who, witnessing for it faithfully, have in the process suffered greatly.

'To be a martyr,' wrote William Barclay in his commentary on the Fourth Gospel, 'was to belong to the royalty of Christianity. There always remained a certain ambiguity about the word "martus"; in both Greek and Latin it could mean "witness" and it can mean "martyr". So there came to be two kinds of martyrdom; "red martyrdom" in which the martyr died for Christ, and "white martyrdom" in which he witnessed for Christ no matter what the cost. Thus Tertullian writes in his treatise *On Flight in Persecution:* "Can Christ claim that you, as a martyren for him, have steadfastly shown him forth?" So we bear in mind that "martyr" was the highest title which could be given to any Christian; but to call a man a martyr did not necessarily mean to say that he had died for the faith; it could mean that he had lived for it.'

Two people who figure in this book come very close to that definition: John Leonard Wilson and Dietrich Bonhoeffer. Wilson lived many years after his sufferings at the hands of the Japanese while Bishop of Singapore during the Second World War. He survived to become eventually Bishop of Birmingham in after times, and a genial and splendid man he was, even though he bore the scars, psychological as well as physical, of his experiences. He did not suffer death; he did not die for the faith; but he showed he was prepared to. And, most certainly, he lived for it.

The case of Bonhoeffer is more complex. It is true that this very great German, a towering Christian figure of this century, died at the hands of his captors, hanged by the Gestapo in 1945. But he did not so suffer because the faith he professed in itself led him to the gallows. What took him there was his membership of a conspiracy to overthrow Hitler. It was his Christian belief which led him to a conviction of the rightness of being a part of the conspiracy which he and others had come to see as a necessary step towards the end of an evil system. Here again, then, was a man who lived out his faith even though it led him into dangerous paths.

There is a third man whose name in this book might well cause surprise – Raoul Wallenburg, the Swedish Diplomat who devoted himself heroically to the rescue of Hungarian Jews. Sent out as an attaché of the Swedish Foreign Ministry in the summer of 1944 to help save as many as possible, he exerted himself to the utmost. The 'Wallenburg passports' as the certificates he used came to be known, saved the lives of many thousands who would otherwise have perished in the death camps. In the January of 1945 he set out under Russian escort, their armies having by then advanced into Eastern Europe, to Soviet Army Headquarters. He was never seen again by the outside world. What happened to him is a mystery. He may even be still alive, an aged prisoner in some Russian gaol.

Yet so long as love of the brethren continues to be a Christian virtue, then surely this gallant Swede deserves a place in any gathering of those who have suffered for the faith. Wallenburg may not have been a Christian in the stricter and narrower confessional sense. But God, after all, may not necessarily be too concerned about such matters. Because he is a God of love it seems highly probable that he would accord such a man as Wallenburg a place at his right hand. And so this 'righteous Gentile', to use the title given him by a Prime Minister of Israel speaking on TV some time ago, features in this gathering of modern martyrs.

But to return to the mystery of the motivation which drives all kinds of people to accept martyrdom in all ages: the conditions in which they do so may vary in detail; but scarcely ever do they vary in principle, and in this there may well be a key to the mystery. It is that in every instance of a martyrdom there is first of all a challenge to be brave for the faith. Often this challenge arises from the fact that they happened to be in a particular place at a particular time, when a hitherto unlooked for challenge came to confront them. Those early Christian martyrs who chose to suffer death rather than submit to what they saw as a Christ denying gesture to Caesar, were in an essentially similar situation to, say, Andrew Kaguru who refused to take the Mau Mau oath in Keyna in 1953. Such people were always in a minority. There must have been many Christians in early centuries who chose to take the outwardly commonsense line of sacrificing to Caesar rather than making an issue of it. After all, it usually meant little more than appearing before a magistrate and sprinkling a pinch of incense on the flame of a

4

small stone altar, accompanying the action with a ritual form of words expressing obedience to a Divine Emperor. The authorities, including the magistrate, usually wanted this to happen without further fuss. Most people took that course, not unlike, in our world, taking an oath in court: an action equally superficial. The Christian could always go away, having discharged his civil obligation, and in peace continue as before, in which case no one would bother.

But to refuse, as a matter of principle, created a frightful scene. The person refusing would be pressed to conform and warned of the consequences of further obstinacy if he or she continued obdurate. Only physical pressure, usually torture, remained, often to the distress of all concerned. There is a dramatic scene in the account of the trial and execution of a young woman, Victoria, a martyr at Carthage in the year 304 during a persecution under the Emperor Diocletian. She has been arrested attending a secret Eucharist. Cross examination before a magistrate follows.

'Why did you celebrate the Eucharist contrary to the Imperial edict?'

'We cannot do without the Eucharist.'

'Who put these ideas into your head?'

'Almighty God.'

'Sacrifice!'

'No!'

'Would you like time to consider?'

'No.'

She is then hung up by her thumbs and asked again.

'Sacrifice!'

'I will not.'

'Scrape her sides.'

As a torturer approaches with the iron claw used for this purpose, the magistrate tries again to persuade her.

'Take my advice, poor woman, spare yourself.'

'No! I have within me the God whom I serve through Jesus Christ.'

And so it continues, until her death in the arena.

There is a striking similarity, even in the dialogue, between this and the case of the Mau Mau victim, Andrew Kaguru and his family. His wife, pinioned before him, is confronted with a choice.

'Take the oath, or we will kill your husband!'

'Never. I am a Christian.'

'We will save you and him, if you will.'

But she continues to refuse, and he is duly killed.

The challenge, then, is always in some way to deny the faith, and the response of the martyr is always to refuse to do so. The motive can derive only from the strength with which the faith is held. Obviously, this is far beyond the norm. How many of us, if faced with some similar situation, would be able to respond with this extreme determination? Clearly, there is something very special here. The power of God is certainly there. It may also be some special quality in the personality of the martyr: an unusual obstinacy, or an exceptional rigidity in attitude. This does not, however, seem to fit universally. Many martyrs may have been gentle people; modest in disposition. The odd thing is that so often they manage, under extreme pressure, to outdo in endurance and courage many people outwardly far more impressive. Martyrs, in fact, do not belong in the same category as the heavily decorated soldier or sailor or airman who has distinguished himself in battle. Their world is totally different. There is here, surely, a manifestation of that strange divine mystery whereby strength seems so often to dwell in apparent weakness. 'To shame the wise, God has chosen what the world counts folly, and to shame what is strong God has chosen what the world counts weakness.' (1 Cor. 1:27.)

So wrote Paul, observing this strange phenomenon, and indeed showing it forth in his own life. Even a physical weakness from which he suffered he endured in the same spirit, seeing in it a check to spiritual pride. 'I was given a sharp pain in my body which came as Satan's messenger to bruise me: this was to save me from being unduly elated.

Three times I begged the Lord to rid me of it, but his answer was: "My grace is all you need: power comes to its full strength in weakness." I shall therefore prefer to find my joy and pride in the very things which are my weakness, and then the power of Christ will come and rest upon me.' (2 Cor. 12:7–9.)

Somewhere in this area, then, lies the motivation which compels some people to martyrdom, given the challenge. What does change, however, is the form which that challenge can take. In the ancient world it could be the power of Rome demanding uniformity of allegiance from its citizens, in such cases as that of Victoria at Carthage, and as with Bonhoeffer in the Germany of the Third Reich. Or it could be an occupying power seeking out what it saw as possibly subversive representatives of a former regime, as with that of Redlich and Sadd, executed by the Japanese. In some instances the martyrdom could arise from a situation of racial conflict, as with Jonathan Daniels, a white man who died in the Civil Rights disturbances in the American South in 1965, or Martin Luther King, who gave his life in the same cause three years later.

Always there are those ready to inflict the martyrdom, and these deserve more interested attention than they usually receive. After all, it is a divine command to care for such people: 'Love your enemies and pray for your persecutors; only so can you be children of your heavenly Father.' (Matt. 5:45), a command echoed by Paul: 'Call down blessings on your persecutors – blessings, not curses.' (Rom. 12:14.)

Most martyrs have done just this. Moreover, not all persecutors have been necessarily wholly evil, a truth often very difficult to realize. Some, however horrific their actions, have been deeply sincere in the conviction that what they were doing was right, as an unpleasant but necessary outcome of their own loyalties. The situation between persecuted and persecutors, and between martyr and inflictor of the martyrdom, can be much more complex than a straightforward confrontation between good and evil. To achieve a full picture of martyrdom it is always needful to try and look at both sides of the situation. Compassion is necessary and proper for all those involved: Hoess, the apparently inhuman Commandant of Auschwitz, under whose regime Maximilian Kolbe, Edith Stein and millions of others suffered, was an affectionate husband and father. When his wife was disturbed by the smell from the crematoria, he was much disturbed. He was also, to judge by his words in his book, *Commandant of Auschwitz*, convinced of his own uprightness. 'I was never cruel', he wrote, 'and I have never maltreated anyone, even in a fit of temper.' He was, too, a person whose whole life had been distorted by the unemployment which in Germany followed defeat in the First World War. His membership of the SS represented for him security and prestige such as he had never previously known. Where then, along the chain of circumstances which led him to Auschwitz, does the blame lie for his condition? Whose is the ultimate sin? The uneasy feeling persists that, then as now, from Auschwitz to Hiroshima, to whatever manmade terror lies ahead of us, the sin is that of us all, collectively.

So to look at the scene in which each of these martyrs suffered is a necessary part of trying to understand them. We have to try and observe the background. For each a different chain of circumstances led them to the final point. Unless the Japanese had attacked in the Far East in 1942 some of the martyrs featured in this book would not have suffered. Unless Amin had been able to seize power in Uganda for a time, Janani Luwum could have continued untroubled in his ministry. Unless there had been a long chain of historical circumstances, beginning with the slave society of days gone by in the deep South of the USA, there would have been no human rights agitation in the sixties and therefore no martyrdom for Daniel or Martin Luther King.

Any martyrdom is at once a tragedy and a triumph. It is also a drama which can only be played out with a full cast: persecuted and persecutors, heroes and heroines, as well as darker figures who step out from various backgrounds of history to do what they have to do. The soldiers who crucified Christ have never been thought of down the ages as evil individuals so much as men under discipline obeying orders. One of them even tried to relieve Christ's sufferings by offering him a soporific drug on the end of a spear. Another came to recognize in the crucified some mysterious quality which he could describe only by saying: 'Truly, this was a righteous man.' So, to try to understand even a little of the phenomenon of martyrdom, all the elements involved in the action, all the people in the drama need to be looked at and, if possible, understood and forgiven. And above all it needs to be remembered that there is an element of mystery about the whole thing. As T. S. Eliot said in *Murder in the Cathedral*: 'A Christian martyrdom is never an accident, for saints are not made by accident. Still less is a Christian martyrdom the effect of a man's will to become a saint, as a man by willing and contriving may become a ruler of men. A martyrdom is always the design of God, for his love of men to warn them and to lead them, to bring them back to his ways.'

It is, of course, an unending story. The sufferings, and no doubt the martyrdoms, of the Christian men and women in the labour camps and places of exile in the Soviet Union's enormous territories are only now beginning to be heard of as information seeps through. Similarly, the fate of some Chinese Christians in the years which have passed since the Communist takeover remains largely unknown. All these must be for the time being happenings in the Church of silence. Their heroic tales can be told, and no doubt will be, in another book of this kind which will become possible when the truth, as it always does, comes out.

1
A DEATH IN THE DESERT

CHARLES DE FOUCAULD, once a fast-living French cavalry officer became a Trappist Monk and eventually a solitary hermit among the Tuareg people at Tamanrasset, deep in the Sahara desert. His life of prayer and contemplation, marked by extreme self-discipline, profoundly impressed those who met him. He was killed by raiding tribesmen in 1916. The Orders of the Little Brothers and Sisters of Jesus, created after his time, were inspired by his life and example.

Almost at the beginning of this century there stands a man whom some words of T. S. Eliot exactly fit: 'The true martyr is he who has become the instrument of God, who has lost his will in the will of God, not lost it but found it, for he has found freedom in submission to God.' Charles de Foucauld died in 1916, almost accidentally shot far away in the Sahara by a nervous youth who was guarding him. Yet he has come to be seen as very much a man of our times, a man for others, a man whose ideas of the Gospel as a manifestation of the double duty of service to God and service to mankind have had profound effects upon Christian action and thinking in subsequent years. As one of his biographers, Elizabeth Hamilton, has said in her *The Desert My Dwelling Place:* 'He anticipated Vatican II in a number of ways – not least in a simplicity of life that, grounded in the Gospels, recalls the early days of the Church. . . . Moreover he looked beyond the Church as an institution to other Christians – and not only to Christians but to Jews and Moslems. . . . He saw all men, without distinction, as children of God, deserving of respect and destined by right of the Redemption to be happy in the same Heaven.'

His story is extraordinary in every sense of the word. Born into wealthy and aristocratic circles, he was brought up after the death of his parents by his maternal grandfather, Colonel de Morlet, in Strasbourg – a kindly man who greatly spoilt his orphaned grandson. When, after the defeat of France in the Franco–Prussian War of 1870 Strasbourg passed into the possession of Germany, the Colonel moved to Nancy, taking the child and his sister with him. So it was in Nancy that Charles de Foucauld was brought up. In the Cathedral there he made his first Communion; but it was also in Nancy that he abandoned his faith, finding the religion in which he had grown up something from which, gradually in those adolescent years, he drew away. Spiritually, he was in that condition when he entered the army, studying first at the élite Military Academy of St Cyr and then, on his passing out he went to the Cavalry School of the French Army at Saumur.

By this time his grandfather had died and Charles had inherited his wealth. He was thus enabled to live to the utmost the indulgent, dissolute life of a wealthy cavalry officer, enjoying every luxury which money could buy, especially food. He became well known among his contemporaries as a gourmand, as a high liver, as a giver of riotous parties. When he passed out of Saumur, at the bottom of his class, his superior officer reported that he appeared to be entirely self-centred in his interests.

The same kind of life-style persisted when he was posted to the Fourth Hussars at Sezanne where, in a nearby town he established a luxurious batchelor apartment, together with another in Paris for use on his leaves. He also furnished this apartment with a woman – Mimi.

He was now launched, it appeared, well into a dissolute life: neighbours complained of the noise of his parties; comrades marvelled at his wealth. And yet, all the time it seemed, other influences were at work within him. Once, for no apparent reason during his time at Saumur, he was discovered wandering in the countryside dressed as a beggar.

And there were those who noticed how, at the height of his life as a high living Hussar Officer it seemed that at times a sadness would come over him; a sense of boredom and self-disgust. It was as though, for all its outward gaiety, his life-style was profoundly lacking in some deeper quality which, even if unconsciously at that time, he was seeking.

When his regiment was ordered to Algeria he soon found himself in trouble over Mimi – the woman whom he had taken overseas with him. Many officers of his kind kept mistresses; but he insisted on calling Mimi the Vicontesse de Foucauld. This the regiment would not tolerate and he was asked to send her home. When he refused, he was himself sent back to France, dismissed from the regiment for misconduct. He settled himself with Mimi at a hotel overlooking Lake Geneva.

This phase did not last long, for soon he heard that his regiment was in action in Algeria in a tribal rising. So Charles rejoined, leaving Mimi for ever and returning to a place which had already begun to affect him profoundly – North Africa, and the desert, with its strange silences, its illimitable spaces and, here and there in its oases, its strange and varied people. He had already begun to study Arabic and Hebrew: he had already begun to be profoundly interested in Islam. His life was beginning to take an entirely different shape, and he had already got through most of the fortune which he had inherited from his grandfather.

The time was ripe for a major change in direction. It came when, moved by a desire to explore what was then the little known land of Morocco, he resigned his commission and, after a period of Arabic studies in Algiers, set off into the dangerous unknown accompanied as guide by a Rabbi called Mardochee, a man who had travelled much in Morocco. Dressed like him, Charles de Foucauld set off into the unknown on what was to prove a dangerous as well as a lengthy expedition. It was to be a time not only of testing for Charles, but also of spiritual development. Travelling in the company of a Jew, and dressed as one, in a land which traditionally regarded all members of that race with contempt, he learned what it was to be persecuted, brutally treated, submissive of necessity without being inwardly humiliated. The faithfulness of the Jews whom he encountered to their ancestral faith was one of the factors which influenced him when he himself turned to the Christian faith once again.

Another profound impression on him was that of Islam, with which he had already made contact and which he had studied closely. The discipline of the followers of Islam, their unquestioning acceptance of the reality of God, their fierce loyalty to their faith, also made a mark upon him. But for the moment his own time of decision had not yet arrived. At the end of the Moroccan journey he returned to Paris where he produced a book, *Reconnaissance au Maroc*, which was widely acclaimed. 'The most important and remarkable journey in Morocco which a European has accomplished for a century or more', wrote one reviewer. He was now, in physical appearance, a totally different kind of man from the self-indulgent cavalry officer of former days. Thin, with dark piercing eyes, he was an arresting figure. Yet the crisis point in his life was still to come.

It came when towards the end of 1886 he walked into the Church of St Augustine in Paris, entered the Confessional of a celebrated spiritual Director, the Abbé Huvelin and asked for instruction in the Catholic faith. The fact was that religion had become a necessity for Charles, an imperative. So many things had happened to him, deep within his soul since first he had crossed with his regiment into North Africa, that he was an entirely different person. Nor was it only the experiences of the Moroccan expedition which had moved him so much. Stirring within him now, in addition to memories of his experiences among the Jews and with Moslems were also memories of his own childhood: the prayers in the house of his grandfather, the church goings, the beauty and tenderness of it all reaching out to him now across the years. He also at this time made the acquaintance

14

of a deeply Christian family. This was the time when, in that same church of St Augustine, he would spend hours praying: 'My God, if you exist, make your existence known to me.'

God did just that. But it was very much in character with Charles de Foucauld that, having accepted the faith and returned to the Church, he decided that he should become a monk. An incident which had strengthened him in this resolve was when he was taken, by a family whom he was visiting, to visit a Trappist Monastery. Austere in life, and vowed to silence, the regime of these Trappists was one of great rigour. And when Charles, on this visit, saw one of the brothers wearing a ragged habit, he understood also that these men were sworn to poverty. He was enormously attracted and, after a brief pilgrimage to the Holy Land, he decided that he himself, after giving all that he possessed over to his sister, would enter the Trappist Monastery of Notre Dame des Neiges – Our Lady of the Snows – high up in a desolate countryside where there was no sound but the wind in the pines.

But even this isolation and extreme simplicity of life was not enough for Charles. He was beginning now that search for extreme poverty, for total devotion to the lives and needs of the very poor which was to last him for the rest of his days. Austerity, for him, was all, the royal road to God. Because of this he decided to leave Our Lady of the Snows and go on to another Trappist House where the life was even more severe – The Priory of Our Lady of the Sacred Heart far in the interior of Syria, a monastery which was little more than a huddle of buildings made of board and clay. And yet even this degree of privation did not satisfy him. He wrote in a letter at this time 'You hope that I have enough poverty. No. We are poor as compared with the rich, but not poor as Our Lord was poor, nor poor as I was in Morocco.' He had been sent to watch by the bedside of a labourer who was dying and this experience made him realize that even in the Monastery they were not as poor as

15

this man, dying in total want. Charles de Foucauld wished in his heart to be likewise.

Some little time after this he left the Order and was, at his own request, released from his vows. The next stage in the pilgrimage of this eternally seeking man was Nazareth in the Holy Land where he attached himself for a time to the Convent of the Poor Clares as a man of all work, living in a hut in the garden. From there he passed to the Convent of the same Order in Jerusalem, where again he lived in a hut, in a garden, overlooking the Holy City the view of which delighted him. Up to now he had been known as Brother Charles, for he was not ordained and had been resisting any pressure to make him a priest. But now this next step became inevitable.

Sent on a mission to Rome by the Abbess at Jerusalem he went, on the advice of his Confessor, back to France to receive Holy Orders and there, in 1901, he was ordained priest and even, for a time, returned to Our Lady of the Snows. But he was still restless. He wrote in a letter to a friend: 'The silence of the cloister is not the silence of forgetfulness.' And in this same letter he outlined what had now become his passionate desire: to return to the Moroccan border and to found a very humble hermitage where just a few monks – because he always hoped that some would join him – would live very simply and would practise a universal charity, always being prepared to share anything they had with whoever should come by, guest or stranger, because all men were brothers. This was the resolve, and this the intention which took Charles de Foucauld back to Algeria. There he established himself at the oasis of Beni Abbes, a place where the great dunes of sand, some of them five hundred feet high, stretched away as far as the eye could see and where, intervening, there was a sand plateau. Here he built his hermitage, in a solitary spot some distance from the oasis itself and here he came to love living in the brilliant light, under the great sky, in the silence. Here for years he was to labour and, constantly, to hope that others would join him. That is why the actual place he constructed was larger than required for the needs of one man. Many visitors came to him, soldiers, travellers, many slaves – for the slave trade flourished in the Sahara in those times – and always the poor; but never any other brothers to join him. Some of his possessions were for a long time still to be found in this place. Among them was an alarm clock, on the back of which he had written 'It is the hour to love God.'

He was constantly busy. 'From 4.30 a.m. to 8.30 p.m.,' he wrote in a letter 'I don't stop talking and seeing people: slaves, the poor, the sick, travellers, and those who come merely out of curiosity. He used to give his home-grown barley and dates to the poor. Nearly always he said his Mass before dawn so that he would not be disturbed. There was a French Military Garrison not far away and he used to be astonished at the number of soldiers who would come into his chapel to listen to him give a reading from the Gospels. Sometimes, when there was fighting in the area, he would go out to a field hospital and be with the wounded. The matter of slaves was a constant concern with him. It was a trade which had flourished for generations in that part of the world which lay on a slave route from the distant South, where they had been captured, up to the Mediterranean coast where they would be sold. It was a traffic which he saw as a plague, as an abomination. Many of the slaves were children. Often these and others came to Charles for sanctuary, and though some he bought and released there was little he could do on a greater scale. One, of whom he became very fond, he called Abdiesus, a name ancient in African Christianity, and this boy he sent to the White Fathers in Algiers. Another was a Negro boy whom he christened Paul and who, as it happened, was to be present when Charles met his death. In 1902 an old Negress, homeless and nearly blind, came to him and Charles baptized her in the name Maria. She was still there at her death in 1923, still in receipt of a small pension Charles had left her.

But Beni Abbes was not to be the place where Charles

reached the end of his journey. It was at another oasis, far to the South of the Sahara, in the region known as the Hoggar, at a place called Tamanrasset that he was to meet his destined end. Before this, he had always wished to renew his journeyings in Morocco; but that country was closed to him and it was at this time that a French Officer, Henri Laperrine, Commander-in-Chief of the Saharan Oases asked him to go and work among the Tuareg peoples of the Hoggar, a proud and fierce tribe. Charles had previous knowledge of these people, because, a few years before, they had assassinated a friend who had been with him at the Cavalry School at Saumur. This man, the Marquis de Mores, had been killed on the borders of Tripolitania, within the area of the Tuareg, who had slain him just as they had a French Military Mission some years before. Charles wrote to a mutual friend when he had moved to Tamanrasset, 'Yes, I am living among the tribes who killed my friend, taking vengeance, avenging him by returning good for evil, trying to give them life eternal. My dear Mores, of whom I think, for whom I pray each day, helps me. In Heaven, in the bosom of eternal life, bathed in a flood of boundless charity, he has only prayer and love for those Moslems who shed his blood and will perhaps shed mine.'

A glimpse of Charles de Foucauld journeying through the desert comes from these times and is evocative of the qualities of this man. By five in the morning the temperature would be rising to 50 centigrade. It would be necessary for each of the travellers in a caravan to drink two and a half gallons of water a day. Once, when travelling with some White Fathers, Charles persisted, as was his custom, in walking with his camel fifty yards ahead of the party as it fought a way across the blinding desert. He had no watch, and so asked one of the Fathers to mark the passage of each hour by striking a metal pot on his saddle, so that Father de Foucauld, wrapt in his prayers, could mark the passage of time. And each time the gong-like sound rang out in the silence of the desert he would turn round, and bow his acknowledgement.

He laboured greatly among the Tuareg, among other things translating the Gospels into their own tongue. At Tamanrasset, which he described as 'a village of twenty homes, right in the mountains, in the heart of the Hoggar', he made his base saying, 'I choose this abandoned place and here I stick'. In a letter to a White Father he set out the principles of his missionary method which was, years later, to bear much fruit, and is still doing so, in the lives of the Little Brothers of Jesus and the Little Sisters of Jesus, who were among the eventual outcomes of his work. 'In countries so poor, where life is simple, the missionaries, if they are not to build a wall between themselves and their flock; if they are not to alienate those whom they hope to attract; if they are not to gain an unpleasant and unevangelical reputation for wealth, will be obliged to live in great poverty.'

And that, of course, was what he did himself. Tamanrasset, now, in these days of air travel, easily visited by tourists, was then utterly isolated and here he chose his hermitage: a place not far from the dwellings of the people, where he could live his own life, always through the years hoping that others would join him. Nobody did, although there was as constant a stream of visitors as there had been at Beni Abbes. He used at this time to think of the White Sisters whom he had known in Nazareth and Jerusalem and realize how much good a female Order could do among the women of the Tuareg if only they would go there. But, as with the brothers he was looking for, none came in his time. So he continued to live his isolated life, alone except for that God whose presence he constantly sought and who, in his tiny, uncomfortable chapel, he worshipped.

The end came for him when a party of Senoussistes, in the March of 1916, invaded from Tripolitania on 1 December of that year. After dark, about seven in the evening, they came to Tamanrasset.

Paul, the slave whom Charles had released years before, and who now lived nearby with his wife and family, had

19

cooked Charles supper and gone home. Charles – 'the marabout' as the Tuareg called him – was sitting solitary in the lamplight among his books and manuscripts and letters. Then a great knocking crashed into the silence. When he opened the door he was seized, dragged outside, tied up and flung to his knees. Paul was dragged from his house and compelled to witness all that followed. The Senoussistes left a young boy armed with a rifle to guard Father de Foucauld while they pillaged the house. Some movement in the prisoner must have panicked the boy because, according to Paul who witnessed everything, seeing the movement and thinking maybe that the prisoner was trying to escape, the boy pulled the trigger and the bullet passed through Father Foucauld's head. It hit the wall behind him, and the hole it made can be seen to this day. A Moslem friend, hearing of the death, wrote to an acquaintance in France: 'Charles the marabout has died not only for all of you, he has died for us, too. May God have mercy on him, and may we meet him in Paradise.'

Nobody, it needs to be said again, had in his lifetime gone to join him. After him, the buildings he had put up at Beni Abbes fell into disuse and ruin until, in 1933, a Frenchman, René Boillaum who had read some of Charles de Foucauld's spiritual writings and been moved by them, went to the place and was inspired. Five young Priests, of whom René was one, settled in an Arab village on the edge of the Sahara, following the Rule which had been written years before by de Foucauld for the guidance of whoever should come after him. There they studied Arabic, ran a dispensary, served the people around them. Scattered during the Second World War, they returned and commenced that new way of life which emerged as the Order of The Little Brothers of Jesus, soon to be followed by The Little Sisters.

The Order has spread worldwide and, though never large in number, it is significant by its presence, and total absorption with communities in many lands. The men and women whom Charles de Foucauld waited for in vain during his lifetime, truly came to him afterwards when the seed which had been growing secretly put forth its growth. So there are Little Brothers and Little Sisters in France, in India, in Vietnam, in Leeds, in Hamburg, in Sardinia, in Algiers itself. All work among people they have come to serve, just as Charles worked among the Tuareg, and they call themselves 'Little' because it typifies their attitude to life and to those whom they seek to serve. So the Father Voillaume, the man who had gone to the ruins at Beni Abbes in 1933, and who became Prior General of the Little Brothers, said later: 'Be little. Little we are before the task we have to accomplish. Little we shall also be in the eyes of men. All our lives we shall remain unprofitable servants, and we must wish so to be dealt with.' But this littleness, as with Charles de Foucault, is a sign of greatness.

Yet the emergence of these Orders is by no means to be seen as the full consequence of the life of Charles de Foucauld. There is more; because his search for God was so unrelenting, his courage in adversity so triumphant, his self abnegation so total, and his sense of the reality of the divine so compelling, he has become a landmark upon that road along which many, in all places and times themselves seek to find God. He is among the company of·martyrs, because he gave his life in this search. Many others have done, because the whole company of martyrs is singularly varied. Few greater contrasts could be imagined than that between this solitary Frenchman of the desert, and the two Americans, a husband and a wife, who died in China in the thirties, John and Betty Stam.

2

CHINA INCIDENT

JOHN AND BETTY STAM, of the China Inland Mission, young, married, and with a baby, met their deaths by beheading at Tsingteh on the Yangtze river in the December of 1934. It was only an incident in the turbulent history of China at that time; but it looms larger when seen against the background, not only of the whole heroic missionary enterprise in that land; but of the continuing story of Christian martyrdom everywhere.

Christianity reached China in the very early years of the faith. There is a legend that St Thomas the Apostle himself travelled there, made some conversions, then returned to Meliapur in Southern India, where he died. But legend moves into history with the appearance in China, or Cathay, as it was called, of the Franciscans in the middle ages. This was at a time when the rise of the Mongols, under Genghis Khan brought terror to Europe and a need to know more of the regions whence these frightening invaders from the east seemed to emerge. Two friars, John of Pian and William of Rubruck made a way to China and brought back some information about the land. They were followed by Marco Polo himself, the great explorer. Eventually, and largely as a result of these approaches, a Catholic Archbishopric was established in Peking, and colonies of Christians appeared at scattered points in China. But, as has happened so often in the Christian history of that vast country, it ended in martyrdom and death as one dynasty succeeded another, and turned upon those whom their predecessors had favoured.

A similar pattern emerged following the arrival of the Jesuits in later centuries. The work of the society survived the collapse of the Ming Dynasty. Their successors, the

Manchus, to some extent permitted collaboration. But even at the most promising period of that development there were not more than twenty missionaries serving the needs of some one hundred thousand Christians. And then persecution came as the missionary enterprise was suspected of being involved with the increasingly rapacious and violent methods of foreign traders. This was always a peril to which a Christian was exposed – to be associated with the actions of 'the foreign devils'. No understanding of the Christian effort is really possible without recognition of this basic fact which continues as a permanent factor throughout the centuries. It has been said that from the middle of the eighteenth century to the middle of the nineteenth persecution of Christians was continuous, breaking out here and there, in this province or in that, according to local feeling. When, for instance, in 1784, four Italian Franciscans, travelling secretly within the country, were arrested, an imperial edict was issued which commanded destruction of all Christian churches in the provinces, the arrest of all European and Chinese priests and the forcible renunciation of the faith by all Christians. There were many martyrdoms, and by the close of the eighteenth century the Christian cause had been virtually extinguished. It is possible now to begin to see something of the vast picture into which the story of John and Betty Stam, fits far away in the twentieth century.

The protestant missions arrived in China at the beginning of the nineteenth century. By then, the Christians in China were a few Catholics, to be found in very small numbers up and down the country. Yet by 1889 there were 37,000 protestant Christians. Many factors had brought this about, including the influence of the missionary zeal implanted in the protestant mind by such men as Wesley and Carey. But there was also the remarkable preliminary work of such men as the great Dr Morrison, the pioneer among Protestant Missionaries to China. An Englishman he set off for China in 1807 and, basing himself at Canton, set himself the task of

24

translating and printing the whole of the Bible into Chinese. When he died in 1834 this task was done, and he had received ten converts. Thus it came about that various Protestant churches, largely from England and America, working in the Treaty Ports and at first not venturing very far inland, went about their work with an extraordinary zeal. They were strongly Bible based, and were aided by the schools and colleges they founded and the medical work they undertook.

But the giant among Protestant pioneers was undoubtedly James Hudson Taylor. Who he was and what he did and what he accomplished are part of the story of John and Betty Stam because, in the fullness of time, they were to live – and die – as part of the organization he founded – The China Inland Mission. The tale of Hudson Taylor, and of this singularly heroic mission, are both illustrations of the truth of the words of Jesus 'For men this is impossible; but everything is possible for God.' (Matt. 19:26.)

Taylor, born in 1832 in Yorkshire, had always wished to be a missionary and it was as such that, in 1853, he went to China as a preacher for the Chinese Evangelization Society. Ill health at first defeated him, and forced him back to England. But, having in the interim studied medicine, he returned to China. His work was dominated by two essential characteristics of his belief: a total reliance upon God and an equally total acceptance of the view that no man could be saved unless he had first heard and then accepted the Gospel. Without, they were lost, and when he surveyed the immensity of China, with its many million people, he needed all his faith and all his courage to set about the task to which he truly believed God had called him. In 1865 he appealed for twenty-four helpers. Two years later he received them. In 1876 he appealed again for eighteen, and these joined him in the work. Five years later he appealed yet again for seventy more, and in 1886 for a hundred and later for a thousand. All were eventually forthcoming and these formed the nucleus of the China Inland Mission.

It was from the first undenominational. For its members

the Bible was supreme. Men and women of the mission, penetrated inland, preaching the Gospel and distributing literature, always encouraging those whom they converted to create churches of their own. The mission was characterized always by the total sincerity and great physical courage of its members.

Meanwhile, the turbulent history of China itself continued. The Boxer rising in the early years of this century brought suffering and death to many. And as the great powers of the world extracted more and more indemnities from the Chinese, and became increasingly demanding of privileges of trade and territory, so hostility to any foreign influence inevitably increased. And though at first, in the years following the rising, it seemed that the Chinese were turning with enthusiasm to the opportunities of education offered by mission schools and colleges, in their desire to equip themselves with Western technologies, the seeds of the conflict which were eventually to result in the total communization of the country by the middle of the century were already being sown. Two casualties of that conquest were to be John and Betty Stam.

Through the times of Sun Yet-Sen, Founder of the Chinese Republic, a Christian and a product of a mission school, to that of Chiang Kai 'Shek through to the Japanese invasions of the late thirties, the Second World War, the rise of Mao Tse 'Tung and the final triumph of communism, the life of China continued to be profoundly and tragically disturbed. It was not a propitious time for missionary endeavour. After the death of Sun Yet-Sen in 1925 the divisions between his successor, Chiang Kai 'Shek, and the growing communist power became more acute. This was a dangerous time for Christians, and attacks on missionaries and church property were frequent. The framework of the events which led to the martyrdom of John and Betty Stam can now be seen.

Betty Stam, the child of American missionary parents – among protestant missions in China the

26

Americans had always been predominant – had studied at the Moody Bible Institute in Chicago. There she met her husband-to-be, and they married when both were in China. Significantly, while she was studying, and not knowing at all what was to come, she had written in a letter to her brother: 'All Jesus' followers have to do, all they can do, is to lift Christ before the world, bring him in to dingy corners and dark places of the earth where he is unknown, introduce him to strangers, talk about him to everybody, and live so closely with him and in him that others may see that there really is such a person as Jesus.'

Her husband, John, sometime later than this, when they were both involved in their work in China, had written: 'In our lives it is well to remember that God's supervision is so blessedly true that any given moment, whether we face suffering or joy, times of intense activity and responsibility or times of rest and leisure, whatever we face we may say, "For this cause came I unto this hour." All our social, church and family background, all of our training, conscious and unconscious, has been to prepare us to meet the present circumstances, and to meet them to the glory of his name. This will bring us to our tasks relieved of shrinking. "For this cause came I unto this hour. Father glorify thy name".'

To place these two passages side by side is to realize indeed what manner of people this husband and wife were. Their mission was at Tsingteh on the Yangtze River, and an examination of the map of China makes plain how isolated they were in this situation. The date was now the October of 1933. The war between Nationalists and Communists was ravaging the country. No one knew what was to happen next; any community could be open to sudden attack, and it required little effort of the imagination to understand how severe must have been the test of nerve and resolution and faith for this man and this woman, together with their baby daughter, to persist in carrying on their work at such a time. They could have taken a safer way but freely, voluntarily they chose what to them was a better way. The degree of faith required to make such a choice can only, in the beholder, arouse an awed respect, 'Then what can separate us from the love of Christ?' asked Paul: 'Can affliction or hardship? Can persecution, hunger, nakedness, peril or the sword? "We are being done to death for thy sake all day long", as scripture says; "We have been treated like sheep for slaughter" – and yet, in spite of all, overwhelming victory is ours through him who loved us. For I am convinced that there is nothing in death or life, in the realm of spirits or super human powers, in the world as it is or in the world as it shall be, in the forces of the universe, in heights or depths – nothing in all creation that can separate us from the love of God in Christ Jesus our Lord.' (Rom. 8:35–39.)

In the early part of December of that year Tsingteh was captured by communist troops. A party of them, early one morning, climbed the city wall and opened the gates to admit the main body. It was a fearful incursion, for murder and looting, after the pattern of war at that time in those regions, were bound to follow. Soon the sounds of fighting, shots and shouting, reached into the Stam's house, where Betty Stam was bathing the baby. There was to be no escape; their house was bound to be looted. Soon, when they heard shouts and knockings at the outer door, they knew that the time had come. The Stams knelt in prayer with their Chinese servants and then, with every courtesy opened the door, and the troops poured in. They wanted money, and they wanted loot. The last presented no difficulties, they could take the contents of the house, as indeed they did. But money was a different matter. They wanted twenty thousand dollars, and demanded that John Stam should write to his mission headquarters asking that this should be sent. He knew perfectly well that this would not happen: it was not within the powers of the mission to do such a thing and, sensing the fearful dilemma which the receipt of the request would place them, he ended his note with the words: 'God give you wisdom in all you do and give us grace and fortitude. He is able!'

It is said that, while these negotiations were in progress, Betty Stam was serving tea and biscuits to the troops who were, at that very time, making it plain that her life and that of her husband would be spared only if the money were to be forthcoming. When the note had been written, John Stam was taken off by the troops. Shortly afterwards they came back for Betty; but the baby was left behind.

When it eventually became clear that no ransom for them was to be paid, they both suffered together. What passed through their minds in that time of waiting; what agonies for the child, what fears for what was to come, above all, what fervent prayers must have gone up from them no one can know. They died, as that other in whom they so ardently believed, had himself done, on a hill outside the town. A crowd had been forcibly gathered to witness the execution. Betty Stam had to watch while her husband was forced to kneel, and then, with a sweep of the sword, beheaded. Then, in the same way, forced to kneel, she also was executed, and her blood mingled with his upon the ground. Meanwhile, back at their house, the baby had been taken by Christian friends and these eventually were able to hand her over to the mission. She was brought up by Betty Stam's parents.

These two, John and Betty Stam, died because of what they were and where they were, Christians in a martyrdom situation required to pay with their lives for their faithfulness to the Gospel to which they were called. Both were young; but of each could it truly be said, 'As for me, already my life is being poured out on the altar, and the hour for my departure is upon me. I have run the great race, I have finished the course, I have kept the faith.' (2 Tim. 4:6–8.)

Years later, in another place in another time, a Polish priest, Maximilian Kolbe, was to do the same, in yet another chapter in the unending history of martyrdom.

3
FRANCISCAN IN AUSCHWITZ

MAXIMILIAN KOLBE, canonized in 1982, perished in Auschwitz in 1941. He chose to die in order to save the life of a fellow prisoner who had been condemned to death. Kolbe's life and witness have been of particular inspiration to Poland, and to Christendom in general.

One of the largest concentration camps established by the SS in the Second World War, Auschwitz in Poland became eventually one of the main extermination centres for Jews, and others. Many Poles suffered there also. Millions of men, women, and children entered through its gates; few ever returned. Details of the deaths of the great majority are unknown. But in some few cases information has survived and the fact that Rudolph Hoess, at one time Commandant, was compelled to write his autobiography early in 1947 while in prison in Poland awaiting trial and eventual execution, has lifted at least one corner of the dark curtain which has covered forever most of what took place.

One of the matters with which Hoess concerns himself in his grim book is the question of escapes. According to him, while this was extremely difficult from most other camps, it was, surprisingly, rather easier from Auschwitz. He wrote: 'Flight was not very difficult: opportunities for escape were many. The necessary preparations were easily made, and it was a simple matter to avoid or outwit the guards. A little courage and a little luck were all that was needed. But when a man stakes everything on one throw, he must also of course reckon that if it goes wrong the result may be his death. But these projects of escape always involved the prospect of

31

reprisals, the arrest of family and relations, and the liquidation of ten or more fellow prisoners.' Sometimes he goes on to say, especially cruel reprisals were ordered. The Commander of the Protective Custody Camp had a particularly horrible way with escapes. He would order indiscriminate arrests to be made among camp inmates and then have these prisoners locked into punishment cells, concrete bunkers, where they were left to starve, without food, water or light, until the end. It was as a result of an escape attempt by a Polish prisoner in Auschwitz that a notable martyrdom took place.

The would-be escaper was Francizek Gajowniczek, a Polish army sergeant. The name of the martyr who suffered as a consequence of his action was Maximilian Kolbe now the Blessed Maximilian Kolbe, canonized on 7 March 1982. Gajowniczek was present, aged 82, during the three hour ceremony in Rome, sobbing throughout as he sat at the front of the huge crowd. Also present were some 300 Bishops and Archbishops, and an Italian woman, Angelina Testoni, whom Father Kolbe was credited with having cured of a fatal illness. There was also a Polish Communist Government delegation, marking something of the deep significance of the occasion to the whole nation in all its many and continuing trials.

The Pope, who was known to have attached particular importance to the canonization, said that Kolbe's actions were a vivid illustration of human dignity. 'His death', he said, 'was a victory over all the system of contempt and hate for man, and for what is divine in man, a victory like that won by Jesus Christ on Calvary.' He emphasized that the Church was proclaiming Father Kolbe both a saint and a martyr, indicating that his death came in bold defence of the Christian faith. Meanwhile in Poland, thousands had travelled to the small town outside Warsaw, Niepokalandow where Kolbe had founded a monastery and the Order of the Knights of the Virgin Mary. Maximilian was Kolbe's name in religion. But he was christened

Raymond, born into a devout Polish Catholic family in 1894. It was said that when he was a boy he had a dream in which he saw the Blessed Virgin, Mary the Mother of Jesus, bearing two crowns, one white, one red. These signified the two forms of martyrdom: the white involving faithfulness, but not death: the red involving death itself. Raymond in his dream was asked to choose. Characteristically, he chose both. There was from the first an ardent quality about this young man which impressed greatly, although some were disturbed by his extreme devotion to the Virgin – extreme even for Poland. He was not strong physically, and his ill health eventually developed into tuberculosis. But this did not lessen in any way the ardour with which he carried out what he felt to be his duty, which was to create and further a missionary enterprise in his native Poland, dedicated to the Blessed Virgin whom he had seen in his dream, and concerned to bring to Christ as many men and women whom he could influence.

He joined the Franciscan Order, and was a lay brother for eight years before ordination. In his enthusiasm, in his fervour, in the intensity combined with simplicity, of his faith, there was something typically Franciscan. Not for nothing has Francis of Assisi, the high-spirited son of a rich father, who became dissatisfied with his worldly life during a serious illness and, after prayer and inner conflict, devoted himself to prayer and the service of the poor, become one of the most cherished saints in modern times. It was Francis who, on a pilgrimage to Rome, was so moved by compassion for the beggars outside St Peters, that he exchanged his clothes with one of them and spent a day himself begging. The experience affected him deeply: then and later he discovered both the joys and the hardships of utter poverty. It was the turning point of his life. On his return to Assisi when he was disowned by his shocked father, he devoted himself to ministering to lepers and spent the rest of his time restoring a ruined church. It was while worshipping one morning that he heard the words of Christ

33

bidding his disciples to leave all. From that point onwards he totally turned aside from personal possessions, put on a garment girded with a cord and set out to save souls. A little band of like minded followers gathered around him. Such were the origins of the Franciscan Order which, although it soon outstripped in size and complexity the simplicities of its founder, always in its essence and in the lives of its members, sought to show forth his Christ-like principles.

So did young Maximilian in the years before 1918. He also formed small groups of devout Christians. They were to be discovered all over Poland by 1922, by which time he had been ordained a priest, and had begun to publish an evangelistic magazine which in a few years achieved an enormous success. Indeed, the success of this and other evangelistic enterprises were so great – for he was a gifted and enthusiastic communicator – that by 1927 he and the large community of Friars which had gathered around him, had created a centre west of Warsaw which was to become one of the largest Franciscan Houses in the world. This was Niepokalanow. By 1930, leaving this work in full swing, Maximilian was in Japan, opening up a similar enterprise there. Six years later he was recalled to Poland. Three years after that, in the September of 1939, the Germans invaded his native land.

The exceptional brutality of the Nazi occupation of Poland is a matter of history. With the exception of Soviet Russia itself, it is possible that no country invaded by German forces in the Second World War suffered to a comparable degree. Quite apart from the fate which befell the Polish Jews which there, as elsewhere, was nothing less than extermination, German rule bore with particular severity upon the native Poles. It was as though that tragic country, which all through history seems to have been singled out for suffering, caught between the two hammers of Soviet Russia on the one hand and Germany on the other, and occupied by both, was once again to re-enact its customary and frightful role of victim. It is therefore a sad injustice to the memory of the millions of Poles who died during this occupation to suppose that the only victims of it were Jews. As it happened, both Poles and Jews themselves suffered almost equally, and both on racial grounds: the Jews as Semites, the Poles as Slavs.

Inevitably, the work which Kolbe had founded at Niepokalanow, being of such prominence, immediately attracted the attention of the occupying power. Many of the people there, including Maximilian himself, were deported to Germany for forced labour. For some reason or other, however, possibly associated with the crazy inconsequence of the times, they were released and returned to Poland.

That would have been the moment, if Maximilian had been at all concerned for his own safety, to have assumed a low profile, trying his utmost not to draw any attention to himself or to his work in the hope that both would be overlooked by the baleful eye of the oppressor. But that was not his way; it was not the way of his followers, nor, for that matter, would it ever have been the way of St Francis. The result was that very soon Niepokalanow became a focal point for help to refugees. At one time there were 3,000 of them, including many Jews, as guests of the Community.

The Nazis did not like this, and kept a close eye on all the activity. A passage which appeared, written by Maximilian himself, in the magazine published by the community gave particular offence to them. 'No-one in the world can change Truth. What we can do is to seek Truth and to serve it when we have found it. The real conflict is an inner conflict. Beyond armies of occupation and the hecatombs of extermination camps, there are two irreconcilable enemies in the depths of every soul; good and evil, sin and love. And what use are the victories on the battlefield if we ourselves are defeated in our innermost selves?' Soon after the appearance of this number of the magazine Kolbe was arrested and taken to prison in Moscow. From this point the Passion of Maximilian began.

Part of deliberate German policy in Poland was the

liquidation of all leadership elements in the population: teachers, doctors, lawyers, leading businessmen, politicians, and, above all, priests. In view of the enormous influence exercised by the Church in Poland then, as now, it was not surprising that clergy should be treated with especial severity. Many priests were arrested, and a high proportion suffered death at the hands of sadistic guards. Thus it was with Kolbe himself. He had entered the prison wearing his Franciscan habit, which immediately aroused the anger of one of the staff. What followed is reminiscent of the classic interrogations and torture of early martyrs of the Church. The guard asked Maximilian if he believed in Christ. When he said that he did he was immediately struck. The question was then repeated many times, and always with the same response and result. How might the words of Christ echo in the mind of Kolbe at such a time: 'How blessed you are, when you suffer insults and persecution and every kind of calumny for my sake. Accept it with gladness and exultation, for you have a rich reward in Heaven; in the same way they persecuted the prophets before you.' (Matt. 5. 11, 12.) And also: 'When you are arrested and taken away, do not worry beforehand about what you will say; when the time comes say whatever is given you to say: for it will not be you that speak, but the Holy Spirit.' (Mark 30, 9–11.)

In the May of 1941 Maximilian was taken to Auschwitz and there branded on the forearm with his prisoners number – 16670. Here a torture of particular refinement awaited him, together with other priests who, because of their calling, were subjected to it. This was something of a concentration camp speciality. It was said to have been developed earlier at the camp at Mauthausen, and was called the 'totensteige': a very steep slope up which, in heat or cold, prisoners already weakened carried stones up one-hundred and forty-eight steps, hour after hour, day after day, year after year. It was, and was meant to be, a killer. At Auschwitz, when Maximilian first encountered it, this took the form of carrying large blocks of stone on a building project. Later, under the direction of an ex-criminal guard known as Bloody Krott, the stones were replaced by large tree trunks, which prisoners had first to cut. All this work had to be taken at a run and was always accompanied by continuous beatings and lashings. Here again Maximilian was singled out for special treatment. The guard commander loaded him with specially selected particularly heavy burdens. When eventually Maximilian collapsed he was flogged as he lay on the ground and afterwards, being presumed to be dead, was thrown aside into the mud of the building site. He might have died then, and that might well have been the most merciful end. But he was instead taken surreptitiously into the camp hospital, such as it was, and there languished a long time.

Both there, and when he was drafted back into camp, it is remembered that he seemed able to conduct himself with singular sweetness and love. In that bestial existence which was camp life, prisoners would struggle like beasts to get such food as was provided. But Maximilian somehow had grace to share such food as he managed to get. He even managed to say, to another priest prisoner who survived and recalled it: 'We must be grateful we are here. There is so much for us to do. Look how people need us.' Few in these camps survived for very long. Suffering, labour, and torture were continuous. So the period, May to July, 1941 would have been a long time indeed for those who had entered Auschwitz with Kolbe. But it was in the July that the end came in sight. There was an escape from the camp – one of those happenings of which Commandant Hoess wrote. The prisoner may have got clean away; but the consequences for those left behind from his particular block were atrocious. All were called from their work and paraded. Twenty were selected for death, a figure later reduced to ten. The sentence upon these ten, intended as a deterrent, was that they should be placed in an underground punishment bunker, and there left until they died. One of those selected was Franciszek Gajowniczek who, when picked out, began crying for mercy, saying that he had a wife and children and wanted some time somehow to see them again. This was the 82-year-old man who sat, sobbing, during the canonization proceedings in Rome in 1982. At this Maximilian, who was standing with others in the ranks, stepped forward and begged that he should be allowed to take the man's place. After some argument it was agreed, the soldier returned to his place, and the ten finally selected, including Maximilian, were taken to the underground cell.

What followed poses in an acute manner the question of how it was that martyrs such as Maximilian were able to summon up the strength and constancy which was with them to the end, and which has survived as a memory of what happened in their final days. Here was a man who was already far advanced in consumption, and who had been weakened by the cruellest of treatment since the time of his arrest. Yet it seems that he was able even in this underground cell, to give leadership and inspiration to the other victims with him to an extraordinary degree. As the long hours passed in darkness, and in steadily increasing hunger and thirst, he led his companions in prayer and praise. Daily, camp guards came to inspect them, with shouts dragging open the doors to see how far the victims had moved towards death. Many cried out for food and for water; some struggled to get out; all were kicked back into the darkness. Maximilian, it is recorded, was never one of these; but continued to offer eternal hope to the end to his companions. Whenever, as the days passed, the guards who came opened the doors, they saw that Maximilian was kneeling in prayer. He would get up as they entered and look quite boldly upon them. Eventually, he was the only person left alive in that frightful place. The bodies of his companions lay around in the darkness. It was decided in the end to dispatch him, and an officer was brought over from the hospital to give him a fatal injection of carbolic acid. So perished Maximilian Kolbe: he who, as a boy, had dreamt of the two crowns, the one red and the other white, and had chosen both.

Hoess records that the Poles, the largest single group of prisoners in the camps until early in 1942, were also the bravest of all those whom he encountered. Many of them were sustained in their courage by a fierce patriotism, strengthened by the conviction that their country would eventually emerge, with the allies, victorious. Their passionate desire therefore was to stay alive. But, behind this ardent patriotism was, without a doubt, the living faith of many of them, rooted and grounded in the leadership of their Church. To give this leadership, as best they may, in the most appalling conditions, was the high duty which many priests in the camps were called. God placed before them this challenge, and it was for them to answer it as best they may. It would be unjust to their memory to suppose that Maximilian Kolbe was the only one who did so. But it is certainly true to say that this gentle Franciscan was among the bravest and most faithful of them all, and that the memory of his courage and his constancy lives on.

So does that of a woman, Edith Stein, who suffered in the same concentration camp within a few months of Kolbe.

4

WOMAN OF THE GAS CHAMBER

EDITH STEIN, a Jewess who became, after her conver-
sion, Sister Benedicta of the Cross, was a woman of
outstanding intellectual gifts. Had she lived she might well
have achieved much academic distinction, as did the famous
Carmelite who inspired her, St Teresa of Avila. But it was
her fate to die in Auschwitz and in so doing to witness
powerfully for her faith.

'One young woman caught my attention, particularly as she ran busily hither and thither, helping the smallest children and the old women to undress. She did not look in the least like a Jewess. She waited until the end, helping the women who were not undressed and who had several children with them, encouraging them and calming the children. She went with the very last ones into the gas chamber. Standing in the doorway she said: "I knew all the time we were being brought to Auschwitz to be gassed. When the selection began I avoided being put with the able-bodied ones, as I wished to look after the children. I wanted to go through it all, fully conscious of what was happening. I hope it will be quick. Good-bye!"'

So wrote Rudolph Hoess, Commandant of Auschwitz, describing the extermination of a transport of Jews. Who was the young woman? The haunting possibility is that it could have been none other than Edith Stein the Jewess who became a Carmelite Nun, Sister Benedicta of the Cross, who perished in that same concentration camp. The year certainly tallies, 1942; so does the conduct of the woman. At Westerbrook in Holland, a gathering point for Dutch Jews awaiting transports, a Jewish man who survived to tell the tale, remembered in after years the remarkable behaviour of a nun.

'The misery in the camp and the excitement among the newcomers were indescribable. Sister Benedicta walked about among the women, comforting, helping, soothing like an angel. Many mothers were almost demented, and had for days not been looking after their children, but had been sitting brooding in listless despair. Sister Benedicta at once took care of the poor little ones, washed and combed them, and saw to it that they had food and attention.'

The identity of the woman mentioned by Hoess can only be supposition. But the account of St Benedicta at Westerbrook is fact. So is the account by a Jesuit Priest of a meeting which he had in the German town of Speyer, before the war, with Edith Stein when she was teaching nearby. He was told, before the meeting, by another priest, that he was going to have a surprise; 'For he had never met anyone whose looks betrayed her race as little as Edith Stein. He was right; for the woman who met us might rather be compared with the statue of Uta in Naunburg Cathedral. This was indeed a very special trait of Edith Stein – she came from absolutely pure Jewish blood and was yet a true German woman. . . .' All these are details, but they are elements to add to the tale of this martyr. For it is one which should not be forgotten; but recalled, and with repentance, always.

Edith Stein was of pure Jewish ancestry, born in Breslau, into a gifted family, strict adherents of their ancient faith. Frau Stein, the mother of Edith, was a woman of outstanding character as well as piety. A widow, with seven children to bring up, of whom Edith was the youngest, she was also required to continue the family business. Her husband had been a timber merchant on a large scale. This was the business Frau Stein had, of necessity, to supervise, as well as continuing the home life of the family. At the same time she practised her faith. As Edith's biographer states, Frau Stein 'kept meticulously all the intricate prescriptions of Jewish religious ceremonial; grace at meals was said in Hebrew, and the pictures with which the walls of her home were decorated represented scenes from the Old Testament. Even in her extreme old age she would keep the Jewish Fasts in all their vigour; where it was a question of serving God she would never have dreamt of allowing herself any mitigations. This strict discipline she bequeathed to her youngest daughter, who needed no other moral education than the example of her mother. . . . There was only one standard of behaviour, which was the Law of God.'

This background needs to be kept in mind in any attempt to understand Edith Stein, for it was the root and ground of her own outstanding self-discipline. It was also the reason why the act of parting, in order to become a Christian, from the faith so firmly practised by her mother, which made that parting, when it came, all the harder to bear. There is another matter of significance here: such outstanding loyalty to their faith meant that Frau Stein, and therefore her family, were required to be different in this respect from a Jewish tendency of their day. In that period, at the close of the last century, long before the Nazi persecution of members of their race were fully integrated, for the most part, to the Gentile world of their time. Many were baptized. Some inter-married with Gentile neighbours. But this was never the way of the Steins. And so something of the determination with which Edith was required in after years to show in relation to her Christianity, may well have had its roots and strength in this earlier example.

She was brilliant at school, passing without difficulty into the University at Breslau and later at Gottingen. But a change had taken place in her thinking which was a sorrow to her mother. Edith had lost her faith. The unreasoning beliefs of childhood were not enough in her developing mind to bring her a sense of the reality of God. So, although she continued, out of love for her mother, to go with Frau Stein to the synagogue, her heart was not in it because belief was no longer in her mind. She confessed in later life that from her thirteenth to her twenty-first year she was, in fact, an atheist.

At this stage of her life Edith was a complete intellectual, interested above all in clarity and precision of thinking and drawn increasingly towards the study of philosophy at its higher levels after preliminary work in the fields of literature and history. From the first, and especially at the University of Gottingen, she seemed to find no difficulty in being accepted in the highest intellectual circles especially among philosophers. A few fellow students did not altogether like her self assurance; but for the most part she was accepted as a person of outstanding abilities. And her quite, reposeful manner soon proved enough to win over those who had begun by criticizing her.

No doubt Edith Stein, without the intervention of a whole series of strange happenings in her life, could have gone on to the calm life of a typical German academic. But God, in his wisdom, had other plans in mind. It is impressive, in viewing her life in hindsight, to see how through a series of events she was brought into contact with deeper experiences, with sorrow, as well as with joy, with testing as well as achievement, until eventually she was led to Christ. The first of these events took place when first she went to Gottingen. Her great wish there was to make contact with the famous Professor of Philosophy Husserl, whose thinking she had been following a long time. It was not possible, however, to pass straight to the Professor in the highly formalized academic society of that time. He had a go-between in a distinguished disciple of his, Adolph Reinach. He, like Edith, was a Jew. But in 1916, when Adolph Reinach was serving in the German Army, he and his wife, Anna, were baptized Christians. One year later Adolph was killed on the Western Front, just past his thirtieth year. Edith, who by this time was intimate with this deeply loving pair, fully expected to find Anna shattered by the tragedy. But what she found, when she attended his funeral after he had died of wounds, was something entirely different. Edith Stein's biographer records that:

'Frau Reinach, it is true, had for a short time been disconsolate, while the first stunning pain lasted. But both she and her husband had been baptized a year before and she soon came to realize that the man she loved was in the peace of God, that his life had reached its goal, and that it fell upon her to bear her loss as her share in the Cross of Christ. Together with this realization a deep peace came over her, which was so strong that it communicated itself to those who had come to console her. Edith, too, experienced it. The impression of this truly Christian attitude was so deep that she still spoke about it to a priest a short time before her own death.' From now onwards the slow process of conversion took place within the mind and heart of Edith.

It was helped further by a contact with another Jewish convert, Max Scheler. This man, although a less stable character than Reinach, opened up to Edith a world which had before been quite closed to her, that of the Church. As she wrote herself: 'Without knowing it I had grown up within the barriers of rationalistic prejudices, which now broke down so that the world of faith suddenly rose before my eyes. It was inhabited by people with whom I was in daily contact, to whom I looked up with admiration.' At least, she thought to herself, this was worth pondering seriously.

But the great influence which turned her finally towards baptism and conversion was yet to come into her life. In the summer of 1921 she was staying on a farm owned by the husband of one of her friends. Alone one night, she went to her host's bookshelves to select something to read before going to sleep. By chance, as it appeared then; by God's design, as it appeared later, she picked up the Life of St Teresa of Avila. The whole of the night she read – utterly fascinated, utterly held. In the dawn, as she laid it down, she said to herself: 'This is the Truth.'

This Teresa whose writing came through with such stunning effect upon the mind of Edith Stein centuries later was descended from an old Spanish family. In 1535 she entered a Carmelite Monastery. Illness for a time required that she should withdraw and return home. But it was after she had gone back to the convent life that she resumed a habit of mental prayer which she had already commenced, although in somewhat desultory fashion. But this soon deepened; she developed a mystic life of great intensity, accompanied by an intellectual vision of Christ. She ruled herself strictly, subjecting herself and, subsequently, her own nuns, to exceptionally severe spiritual discipline. In 1562, when the Convent of St Joseph was founded at Avila, she wrote her famous *The Way of Perfection*, and, not long afterwards, her *Life*, a spiritual autobiography. This remarkable woman, in intellectual power and self-discipline strangely resembling Edith Stein, whom she so much influenced, devoted most of the rest of her life to urging upon the Carmelite Order a primitive rule which was in sharp contrast to that which, by that date, the rest of the Order customarily lived by. She encountered great opposition, suffered many things, and died in 1582. She was canonized in 1622. Her character, as a woman of strong resolution and much practical ability marked all that she did. But it was as a spiritual writer that she was of lasting influence and is to this day. She approached the life of prayer in an almost scientific manner, charting such unaccustomed fields as the ways in which, through meditation, an individual may approach a mystical marriage with Christ in spirit and in truth. It is not difficult to see how profound would be the influence of this approach to such a highly intellectualized personality as Edith Stein.

Edith became a teacher in a Convent School in Speyer, run by the Dominican Order. There she was to remain for a further eight years, not as a nun; but as one who was permitted to live the Convent life, and to take part in the daily devotional discipline of the place. An interesting memory of her time there, reminiscent of the manner of living of Teresa of Avila, survives. 'She mortified herself severely, especially with regard to food and sleep; she was always the first in church in the morning. In the beginning she took her place in chapel with the other secular staff behind the girls; but her desire for recollection and for being near the altar led her to ask to be given another seat. So she was assigned a special, velvet covered kneeling bench within the Sanctuary in front of the nuns, which she did not even have to leave for receiving Holy Communion, a fact commented on by some of her pupils. There she would spend every day long hours in prayer, kneeling upright and motionless like a statue.'

But now events were taking place in the world which were to have profound effects upon her. In the January of 1933 Hitler became Chancellor of Germany, and the series of events which led to the rise of National Socialism, the persecution, and eventual attempt at extermination of the Jews, and ultimately World War II, began. These events were reflected in the private life of Edith Stein. Her mother, whom she had been accompanying to the synagogue regularly throughout this period, found it increasingly difficult to carry on the family business. Eventually she was forced to sell, and even then, such was the anti-Semitic feeling that even the local Christian church was reluctant to help. The eventual parting between mother and daughter, although Edith had contined to be of practical help to the very last, was painful in the extreme.

The old lady could never understand, from the profundity of her Jewish faith, why her youngest and favourite daughter should be turning away from her in this way. But it had to be. Edith had decided to become a nun, taking life vows. This was a secret intention which she found it extremely difficult to communicate to her mother. But eventually the hour had to come. 'On the first Sunday of September I was alone with my mother at home,' she wrote, 'she was sitting by the window with her knitting, and I close to her. Then suddenly came the long expected question: "What are you going to do with the Sisters at Cologne?". "Live with them." Now there was a desperate resistance. My mother did not stop working, her knitting wool became entangled; with trembling hands she was trying to unravel it. I helped her with it, while the discussion between us was going on.'

It seemed at this time that God was trying the resolution of Edith to the very uttermost. Her mother was suffering acutely from the changed atmosphere of all around. She was old and she was afraid. And at this very time, it seemed, her daughter was to leave her. But so it was to be. Edith entered the enclosure of the Carmelites in Cologne in the October of 1933. Henceforth she was to be known as Sister Benedicta of the Cross. The final parting with her mother had been terrible. For the last time she went with her to the service in the Synagogue, and on the way there tried to console her. That night, Frau Stein, as her daughter remembered, covered her face with her hands and began to weep. 'I stood behind her chair and placed her silver-white head against my breast. So we remained for a long time, until she let herself be persuaded to go to bed. I led her upstairs and helped her undress. Then I continued to sit on her bed till she herself told me to go to sleep. But I do not think that either of us had any rest that night.' It was as if Christ himself had placed his Cross at the very centre of their relationship.

But there was another, and a greater Cross to come. Pressure upon the Jews increased in severity, with the passing of the Nuremburg Laws. Sister Benedicta, although a Christian was racially a Jewess, and as such was marked down in official records. In view of this, and of other pressures, the nuns sent her from Cologne to another Carmelite Priory at Echt in Holland so as to be, as far as was possible, at some distance from the acute persecution of the Jews then raging in Germany itself. But Edith did not forget the sufferings of her own people. In prayer, in letter writing, by any means available, she exerted herself on their behalf. Her sister Rosa, who by this time had herself become a Christian, came to Holland and lived near the Convent, so that she and Edith were able to meet daily.

48

Then in 1941 Edith learnt that one of her brothers and his whole family had been taken to a concentration camp. It was a sign for her that, unless something very special took place to prevent it, her own end could not be far away. But the nuns at Echt had been very active in trying to make it possible for Edith and her sister to go to Switzerland, and had applied for passports for the two. Edith and Rosa were both summoned to Gestapo Headquarters. This was the point at which the extraordinary stubbornness, the inexplicable obstinacy of the ultimate martyr, showed itself. As she walked into the building, instead of greeting the Officer behind the desk with the customary 'Heil Hitler!', she cried 'Praise to Jesus Christ!' She left the building with the yellow star of Jewry stitched to the clothes of herself and her sister.

At five in the evening of 2 August 1941, when the Sisters of her Convent had gone into Choir, two officers arrived in the parlour of the Mother Prioress demanding to see Sister Benedicta. The Prioress resisted them as long as she could; but inevitably Edith, who was joined by her sister, was taken through a group of angry people who had gathered outside, to the police van which had been waiting. Three days later the nuns at Echt had a telegram from Edith asking for warm clothes, rugs and medicine to be sent to the Concentration Camp at Westabrook where they had been taken. With other nuns, she remained for some days, and it was here that the Dutch businessman noted the singular composure with which Sister Benedicta went about among the children. She had become, as another who noted her there wrote, 'Truly a mother – tending little children whose natural mothers neglected them; a sorrowful mother, suffering with and for her children, who, like herself, would soon be driven into the gas chambers to be liquidated like vermin.'

One glimpse further of Edith Stein, Sister Benedicta of the Cross, survives. On 7 August it was one of her former pupils who, standing on a station platform at Schifferstadt, the place from which Jewish transport set off to the death camp, heard herself called by her christian name. She looked towards the voice and recognized Edith Stein, her former teacher, standing at the window. Edith said: 'Give my love to the Sisters. I am travelling eastwards.'

On 9 August 1942, Edith Stein, together with her sister Rosa, entered the gas chamber at Auschwitz. Whether she was in fact the woman whom Commandant Hoess noticed, must forever remain a mystery. But that Edith Stein – Sister Benedicta of the Cross – had gone the way of a martyr, is a fact.

So, far away, at the other end of the world, two very unassuming young men were, unknown to themselves, about to do the same.

5

TWO MODEST MARTYRS

ALFRED SADD, of the London Missionary Society, and VIVIAN REDLICH, of the Bush Brotherhood, never knew each other. Both were unassuming men who served Christ with the simplicity which was part of their natures. Both died for the faith, one in the Gilbert Islands in 1942, the other in New Guinea in the same year.

As the years have passed since the Second World War it is not easy to realize how enormous its impact on many communities, places, and persons, was the Japanese on-slaught on the Far East following Pearl Harbour. Long prepared, it was an attempt to create a whole new sphere of influence. The geographical areas covered were prodigious in extent. From New Guinea to Singapore, from the Philippines to islands of the Pacific, an entirely new threat suddenly appeared, like an armed man bursting into a room. Japanese fleets appeared on many an horizon, their soldiers landed on many a shore, their aircraft swept over, and for a long time dominated, many a sky. Australia itself for a time stood in danger of invasion, until American naval victories in mid-Pacific checked the advance.

Such 'old, unhappy, far-off things, and battles long ago', have faded into history. More enduring has been the memory of the impact upon many private lives of what happened. There were many heroic acts; no doubt there were many cowardices as well. There was much suffering; there was much trial of faith and hope; there was much death. But also, here and there amid this huge welter of happenings, there were some Christian martyrdoms.

With so many Christian communities scattered across the Pacific area it was inevitable that there should arise confrontations with the new conquerors. Yet it must be said that for the most part the antipathy which Japanese forces showed to some Christians they encountered in the course of their invasions, was based very largely upon their hostility to them as representatives of enemy powers. The Japanese military were not the first, nor the last, to confuse patriotism with religious faith. Those who in the ancient world demanded of their citizens that they should sacrifice to the Emperor were doing something not very different from these Japanese troops who saw as a hostile act any manifestations of faith on the part of those whom they sought to conquer. Therefore, since looking at the motivation of the persecutor should always be a part of any compassionate recognition of the sufferings of the persecuted, it is right to bear in mind that it was his own kind of patriotism which lay behind the action of many a Japanese, however cruel, and however unjustified.

Among the many Christians caught up in this Japanese invasion, some were in prominent positions, like Leonard Wilson, Bishop of Singapore. But others were obscure heroes and heroines. Two very modest figures to whom, totally unexpectedly, and entirely improbably, the splendour of a martyrs crown was to be given, were Vivian Redlich and Alfred Sadd. They could never have known each other, and the places of their martyrdom were separated by many thousands of miles. The unifying factor in both cases is that they died for the faith. The place of the martyrdom of Alfred Sadd was far out in the Pacific on the Island of Beru among the Gilberts. Before the War these were British Colonies, and, thus lay entirely at the mercy of the first Japanese to descend upon them. Beru was typical of those idyllic places where the warm wind rustled palms, and the great rollers of the Pacific beat off-shore outside the lagoon. To Alfred Sadd and his fellow missionaries of his own day, and those before him, it could have with truth have been said;

Brothers, we are treading
Where the Saints have trod.

The London Missionary Society, in 1795, had first brought Christianity to these islands. This was a body representing Congregationalists, as they were then known, Anglicans, Presbyterians and Wesleyans. They had combined to send twenty-nine missionaries to Tahiti, all acting on the principle that there should be no form of denominationalism in their witness, and that every missionary should be free to follow the customs of his own tradition. John Williams, a Londoner, is a striking example of one of these pioneers and was himself to suffer martyrdom just as Alfred Sadd was to do. Williams in 1817 sailed for Eimeo, one of the Society Islands near Tahiti where he opened a chapel and published a Code of Laws. Five years later, he went on to the Cook Islands, translating parts of the Bible into the Raratongan language. Thence he pressed on into the so-called Friendly Islands where, in 1839, at Dillons Bay, Erromanga, he was killed and eaten by the natives who had been angered by cruelties inflicted on them by passing sailors. His death, when news of it reached England, made a great stir and inspired much subsequent missionary activity. To this day, the ship which carries agents of the London Missionary Society around the Islands is still called the John Williams and is the successor to many vessels which have sailed under the same name and in the same cause before it.

So Alfred Sadd, of the London Missionary Society, went to Fiji in 1933. He, in his turn, sailed on the John Williams of the day, working out from Suva to the Islands. Eventually he went to Beru and was based there. This was a long way from his homeland and from his church in Maldon in Essex where he had been ordained. Before that he had been a boy at the Leys School in Cambridge: a fairly simple, wholly uncomplicated character who like doing things rather than thinking about them. His was the faith that shone by

53

example, an entirely uncomplicated kind of devotion which led him naturally to love others, and to serve them. The kind of work he was involved in at Beru was entirely to his taste. He was good with his hands: he could build and repair houses, he could maintain boats, he could help in the Mission Surgery. And always he could preach his simple Gospel, which he did. All in all he was a simple soul. It is scarcely possible to imagine a less probable character to play the dramatic role of a man destined to die heroically for the faith. But God, it seems, does not choose the most striking persons to fill the parts in his great drama. He can call upon a brilliant Edith Stein to die for him: he can do the same for a glittering personality such as Dietrich Bonhoeffer. Yet he can include simple souls, such as Alfred Sadd. As Paul says: 'To shame the wise, God has chosen what the world counts folly, and to shame what is strong God has chosen what the world counts weakness.' (1 Cor. 1:27.)

The Japanese came to the Gilberts in 1942. They arrived on Beru in August of the same year. It is not difficult to conjure up the scene: the naval vessels which had brought the landing party riding off-shore on the blue ocean: the launches putting off from them as the natives on land watched in silent fear their progress. As a general rule the conduct of such Japanese parties was overbearing to a degree, and the purpose of intimidation quite clear. The number of known atrocities which were later revealed, such as the mistreatments of the Chinese population in Singapore, is great enough to make it certain that there were many more unknown atrocities. Rumours of them had already spread far enough to give rise to warnings of what local populations should expect. White people among them especially had been advised to get out before the invaders arrived.

That is an important point in the story of Alfred Sadd. He could have fled; he could have abandoned the people whom he had been trying to serve. But he chose to stay, together with other Europeans, so that his martyrdom was ultimately a matter of personal choice. It is possible that he may have had some inkling of what was to be because earlier in the year he had written in a letter: 'I have a feeling that God has something bigger than this he intends me to do. I hope and pray I shall be found faithful.'

It was a common practice of the Japanese to endeavour to humiliate white officials and other citizens in the eyes of the native populations. The enforced march to Changi Prison of the white inhabitants of Singapore is a case in point. They did the same thing in Hong Kong. But here, on this island, they first gathered together the native population in the church. Alfred Sadd had already been arrested, together with other Europeans. There is something evocative of the ancient practice of requiring people to sprinkle incense upon an imperial altar in the days of Ancient Rome – a practice which led to so many martyrs among those who refused – in the fact that now, these Japanese required of Alfred Sadd that he should walk upon the Union Jack. This he refused to do. It is a point at which patriotism and Christian faith become inextricably combined. What passed through his mind at this point we can obviously never know, just as we can never really understand what motivated those earlier martyrs. A common factor could well be an unwillingness to acknowledge any power greater than the Christ whom they sought to serve. It was an action showing a determination not to show weakness on any issue on the part of those who in their own lives were trying to serve Christ. So Alfred Sadd refused to walk on the flag. With others he was taken away to another island, Tarawa, scene of a huge battle in later years. On the beach of that island, Alfred Sadd was beheaded.

One month before he suffered on the Island of Beru another martyrdom was impending thousands of miles away to the north of Australia, in New Guinea. There also the Japanese tide had flooded and the region was to know terrible sufferings before that tide was eventually turned back. The martyrdom impending was that of a young Anglican Priest, a member of the Bush Brotherhood, Vivian Redlich. But his was no isolated case, or even a very special

55

one. There were many Christian martyrs in New Guinea, men and women. In the area one hundred and eighty-eight Roman Catholics, twenty-four Methodists, fifteen Lutherans, and nine Anglicans suffered for the faith, many of them in horrible circumstances. Fourteen Brothers of the Roman Catholic Society of the Divine Word, eighteen Sisters from the Missionary Sisters, Servants of the Holy Spirit, together with their Bishop and six other Priests, all working on the northern coast of New Guinea were arrested on suspicion of passing information about Japanese military and naval activities over their radio transmitters. All were arrested and put on a ship together with a further number of priests, sisters and Protestant missionaries. After their vessel had put to sea, all were shot; having first been hauled up, blindfolded, into the rigging by their hands. That was in the early part of 1943, some months after Vivian Redlich suffered, and yet other murders of mission workers had taken place in the intervening time. And, since it is not possible to tell the story of all, it is at the same time to do honour to all be endeavouring to tell his.

Vivian Redlich resembles Alfred Sadd at least in one characteristic; he was a simple and modest man. His childhood home had been in a Leicestershire village where his father was rector. After his own ordination he had been serving as a curate at St Johns, Dewsbury Moor in the Diocese of Wakefield when he heard, through an Australian bishop, who had come to speak, about the Bush Brotherhood. This, founded in 1897 to preach the Gospel and administer sacraments to members of the Anglicans in the Outback of Australia, had an immediate appeal for him. The brothers operated over enormous distances in Northern Australia, living simply and hard, ministering to sheep farmers and others living scattered over those regions. So Vivian found himself, when he had offered for the Brotherhood and been accepted, working in the Rockhampton Diocese of Central Australia. That was in the mid-thirties. Then, in 1940 he volunteered for work in New Guinea and found himself eventually at a place called Sangara, on the south coast. A description of his work there is reminiscent of that of Alfred Sadd on Beru. Vivian Redlich also was a man who liked to work with his hands: he could make old cars go; he could build, he could put things together and take them apart again. The very font which he used for baptisms he made out of copper with his own hands.

In the June of 1942 he was ill, and withdrawn by his Bishop back to Diocesan Headquarters at Dogura; but he had promised his people that he would return, especially as by this time the Japanese invasion was in progress. We know now that he did return, and that he went to his death in so doing. Were it not that a government doctor left an account of what happened, the details of his fate might never have been known. This man, a Roman Catholic, himself had escaped from the Japanese, helped in doing so by one of the members of the very Mission at Sangara where Vivian had been working before his temporary withdrawal. This doctor was now surprised to be told that Redlich was back in the area and hiding nearby. It turned out to be true: the doctor discovered Vivian hiding out on the side of a hill, with local people keeping a look out for him to give warning of any hostile approach. In the course of his account of what had happened Vivian revealed the crisis of conscience which he had lived through. He had come back with the Mission boat in order to land supplies nearby during the night, and then, when this task was done, he had to decide whether, as he was perfectly entitled to do, he would return with the boat to the ship. He must have known what were the consequences of staying. He stayed.

After that, very much alone, he went back to Sangara, saying to the natives who had gathered around: 'I am your Missionary. I have come back to you because I knew you would need your Father. I am not going to run away from you. I am going to remain to help you as long as you will let me. Tomorrow is Sunday. I shall say Mass, and any who wish may communicate.' The doctor was with him that night, sleeping in the shelter on the side of the hill. At dawn Vivian told him that he was going to the church to say Mass as he had promised. He was just about to set off when a native hurried in with a warning to both of them to go at once because they had been betrayed to the Japanese by a local man, and that they were even then on their way to them. It would still have been possible for Redlich to flee. But he said, as the doctor later testified: 'Today is Sunday. It is God's day. I shall say Mass. We shall worship God.'

During the Service, the doctor later testified: 'The dense silence of the jungle was broken only by the sound of the Priest's voice praying for his people. Then came the rustle of movement as those bare brown feet moved nearer the altar at the time of Cummunion. He who was about to go down to his own bitter Gethsemane and passion offered up for the last time before the throne of God for his people the saving sacrifice of Christ. As the sacrifice of Christ had its justification on Easter Morning, so too in God's own time will the sacrifice of his loyal and devoted Priest, Brother Redlich.' After the Service the doctor had to make his own escape. Vivian as was equally his duty, remained among his own people. There, shortly afterwards, the native who was betraying them to the Japanese came and took him, together with the Mission's nurse, a girl called Marjorie Brenchley and the teacher, Lilla Lashmar. Another Priest, Henry Holland was likewise taken. So was a teacher called John Duffill and a Papuan Evangelist called Tapiede. This party was handed over to the Japanese and all were beheaded on the beach. Also, about this same time, the fiancée of Vivian Redlich, an Australian nurse called May Hayman, together with a teacher called Mavis Parkinson, and a party of Papuans with whom they had fled for hiding into the jungle, were ambushed by the Japanese. All were killed.

So, for a time at any rate, silence fell upon the scene. It was not until after the war that the full extent of all these martyrdoms became plain. Some, no doubt, died in terror, all in anguish; but all faithfully, and none more so than that

58

modest man, Vivian Redlich. How it would have astonished him – how, maybe, it does astonish him – that his name, that of so modest a man, should be in the Book of Martyrs at St Pauls.

Another – and better known – victim of the Japanese invasions was Leonard Wilson, Bishop of Singapore.

6

THE MAN WHO FORGAVE

LEONARD WILSON, Bishop of Singapore at the time of the Japanese invasion, has been described as a 'Confessor', that is, one who stood steadfast for his faith in face of great suffering. In the twentieth century he lived as one who, in the early Church, would have been called a 'White Martyr': one who did not lose his life but lived it nobly in the face of cruel trials. His oft told story is re-told here, for the benefit of a new generation who were not alive in his times.

The writer of these words must here for a moment become personal and tell of something which happened to him in order to make plain what happened to John Leonard Wilson, Bishop of Singapore in the days of the Second World War. In the late sixties I travelled as interviewer with the BBC Film Unit which was sent out to Singapore, to film the story of this man. When the time came for Wilson to arrive we gathered at the airport to await him. A considerable crowd had already begun to assemble, comprised largely of quite elderly Chinese and Malay men and women.

Eventually the plane arrived and out of it emerged about the most unlikely person, in appearance, to be a Christian hero and martyr as could possibly be imagined. He wore a grey suit, a shabby hat, and had a straggly grey beard. When he entered the arrival lounge he was obviously surprised to see the crowd awaiting him. One of them, a Chinese woman, moved forward, knelt at his feet and kissed his hand. He was very moved and said 'My dear . . .', lifting her to her feet. The woman's gesture indicated something of what he had meant to many people in years past. What he did not mean, in times present, was shown by the attitude of a young policeman who was annoyed at the disturbance which this arrival had caused at the already congested airport. 'Who is this man?', he asked indignantly. He was told that he had been Bishop of Singapore in the last War. The young policeman looks blank. 'What war?' he said with brusque indifference, 'and what Bishop?'

It was a measure of how soon great events are swallowed up in history and erased from the memories of men. That policeman would not have been born in the days when Leonard Wilson suffered and witnessed for the faith in that city of the Far East. But his story needs to be remembered and kept alive, because it is truly that of a plain man who, called upon by a totally unexpected turn of events to witness for the Christ he strove to follow, did not fail in the hour of trial. His ashes rest now in Birmingham Cathedral, and the stone above them says briefly that he was a 'Confessor for the Faith'.

What does that mean? In the Christian experience it has always meant something special. When Peter says to Jesus 'You have the words of eternal life; and we have believed, and have come to know, that you are the Holy one of God', (John 6.69), he was confessing, that is, boldly making an assertion of his personal belief. In the early Christian years, when the Church was subject to much persecution, to be a confessor meant to be one who suffered in making an act of witness for the faith but who did not, in so doing, suffer actual martyrdom. A confessor, in fact, was a 'white' martyr.

Wilson's life before fate decreed that he should clash with the Japanese occupying power in Singapore, followed a development so normal as to make it all the more extraordinary that, when the crunch came, he should have been empowered to act in so heroic a manner. The son of a clergyman, he went to St John's College, Leatherhead, then to Oxford, then to Wycliffe Hall Theological College and was ordained in 1924. He was a missionary in Egypt towards the close of the twenties and then, after some years as a clergyman in England, went east to become Archdeacon of Hong Kong. He was made Bishop of Singapore in 1941.

When Japan invaded the British, Dutch and American areas in the Pacific, many famous places fell into Japanese hands. It was long thought that Singapore, the great island fortress would stand firm. But events transpired very differently. The Japanese came overland down through the Malayan jungles until eventually they stood before the gates of Singapore itself. Crowded with refugees adding to the number of its already congested population, desperately short of water, the city surrendered in the February of 1942. The whole population, civil as well as military, fell into the hands of the invader and was in some cases treated with great brutality, the Chinese suffering with particular severity.

It was an anxious time for the Bishop who, by that time, had been in office just a year, and suddenly found himself faced with a mass of responsibilities and the pastoral care of a large and frightened community. When I was in Singapore with Wilson all those years afterwards, and we sat in what had been his comfortable house in a tree shaded avenue, he told me how the situation had developed. Military prisoners were taken away to Japan's Prisoner of War Camps. The native population was rigorously controlled. For the Europeans, however, conditions were at first not as bad as might have been expected. The Cathedral of St Andrews in the centre of the city was allowed to continue services. One of the Japanese officers, himself a Christian, used personally to attend the services although, as the Bishop told me later, there was a time in the early days when he had to make it perfectly plain that the Cathedral, as a Christian place of worship, was not subject, and would not be subject, to Japanese control. Congregations were very large, and the care of them, and the leadership involved, a stern challenge. And then, after some months of this state of affairs, the Japanese decided to intern all Europeans in Changi Prison.

This was, as it still is, a grim looking complex rather like a huge fortress, several miles outside town. To it men, women and children of the white community were marched to begin years of close confinement, all sorts of people who had been, for the most part, a privileged élite.

In this prison, as it was shown to me by Wilson years later, there was still the large cell where the Bridge Club would meet, there was still the great wall separating the women from the men, and the yard where husbands and wives could hear each others voices but never meet. During this time Wilson himself was deeply involved in the attempt to relieve conditions, which were becoming very severe, for the civilians left behind in Singapore itself. There was considerable hunger and much poverty, and a great need for financial help. In these circumstances the Bishop felt it right to take the lead in collecting money and other supplies for these needy people, and this was in fact done very successfully. But it had dire results.

It so happened that, after almost a year of Japanese occupation, some of their ships were blown up while in harbour. It could only have been sabotage, and was so: an Australian Unit, it emerged later, had been responsible.

The Japanese reacted fiercely. Not knowing how this blow had been administered, and determined to find out, they looked with especial suspicion upon the European community, seeing in it the most likely source of leadership. Their Military Police took over the prison at Changi because it was there, they thought, that there was some kind of radio link sending information to the outside world. There was another reason for their anger, also. Sensitive to any possibility of opposition to their regime they were concerned to put down any manifestation of anti-Japanese feeling some of which, had indeed begun to show itself in Singapore. Here again the finger pointed to the European community. Was there a leader amongst them? What was the real nature of this organization which, as well they knew, had been collecting money, supposedly for the needy in

Singapore? Their eyes fell upon the undoubted leader of this, as of other enterprises – the Bishop.

In order to extract from him the information which they were convinced he possessed they took him to Secret Police Headquarters in Singapore City, housed in the YMCA building in the centre of town. I went there with him on that visit in later years and even then, at that distance of time, the place clearly affected him deeply. From the window of the room where I interviewed him could still be seen the blooms of the Flame of the Forest flowers growing outside in the garden. He told me how the sight of that flower had kept him in mind of God's good world throughout the period of his trials. It was there, too, that the Chinese woman who had knelt as he had arrived at the airport, told of her own imprisonment there and of the tribulations which had befallen many other Christians at that time in that place. But the chief of them without any doubt was Wilson himself.

He was interrogated and beaten with very great severity for days on end. He knew all the time that he simply did not have the information which they wanted, although the more he asserted this the greater became their pressures and the crueller their tortures.

And now it was as though the whole spiritual stature of the man impressively increased. The fundamentally plain man was enabled, in the power of Christ, to rise above his circumstances to great heights of spiritual power and truth. This was when, in fact, he became a confessor for the faith. In a radio talk which he gave, after the war, speaking of those times, he said in the middle of that torture they asked me if I still believed in God. When by God's help I said 'I do', they asked me why God did not save me I said 'God does save me. He does not save me by freeing me from pain or punishment; but he saves me by giving me the spirit to bear it.' When they asked me why I did not curse them, I told them it was because I was a follower of Jesus Christ, who taught us that we were all brethren. I did not like to use the

65

words, 'Father, forgive them.' It seemed too blasphemous to use our Lord's words. But I felt them, and I said, 'Father, I know these men are doing their duty. Help them to see I am innocent.' And when I muttered, 'Forgive them,' I wondered how far I was being dramatic and if I really meant it, because I looked at their faces as they stood around and took it in turns to flog, and their faces were hard and cruel and some of them were evidently enjoying their cruelty. But by the grace of God I saw those men not as they were, but as they had been. Once they were little children playing with their brothers and sisters and happy in their parents' love, in those far off days before they had been conditioned by their false nationalist ideals, and it is hard to hate little children. But even that was not enough. There came into my mind as I lay there the words of that Communion Hymn:

Look Father, look on his anointed face,
And only look on us as found in him;
Look not on our misusings of thy grace,
Our prayer so languid, and our faith so dim;
For lo! between our sins and their reward
We set the Passion of thy Son our Lord.

'And so I saw them', he went on, 'not as they were, not as they had been, but as they were capable of becoming, redeemed by the power of Christ, and I knew it was only common sense to say "forgive".'

There was no immediate happy end to any of this experience. It was true that eventually the Secret Police ceased their torturing and gave up the attempt to extract information from Wilson. But they kept him in prison and it was a long time before he was returned to Changi. He remained shattered in health as a result of his experiences for a long time: it is even arguable as to whether he ever fully recovered.

It used to be said, that among the Japanese prisoners who, after the war, Wilson prepared for Confirmation, there was one whom he recognized as a man who

had been one of his torturers at the Kempitai Headquarters in the YMCA building. That may well have been
the case. All I can say is that I did not find any evidence of
it while I was in Singapore with him, nor did he himself
speak of it. But something more remarkable did happen at
that time. This was the arrival, unheralded and unexpected,
at the Hotel where we were all staying, of a Japanese
Professor from the University of Tokyo. He was an affable
and kindly little man who had come all that way in order to
have what was clearly to him the sheer joy of looking upon
Wilson again. This was the man who, as a Japanese officer in
the forces of occupation, had attended services at St Andrews
Cathedral. In that white building, set among a wide expanse
of lawn with the sea on one side and the traffic circulating
around on the others, I interviewed the two of them: the
former Bishop, the former Japanese officer, by then both
marked by the passage of time and yet united in a true
Christian love and fellowship. As we sat there, within the
bare pews, the Press gathered around, it was possible to feel
that here, in this encounter, was something on both sides, in
both men, representing the triumphant power of Christian
love. There was a strong impression that both of them had
both passed through so many changes and chances of
fortune, had both known so many experiences, that at the
last they had emerged towards an understanding of the only
thing that ultimately mattered, the love of God in Christ
Jesus our Lord. It used to be said that in his old age St John
used to exhort his followers, over and over again, to love one
another until, in the end, it seemed that he had nothing else
left to say. But maybe that is all that is really worth saying, in
the final analysis. 'Dear friends,' said St John, 'let us love one
another, because love is from God. Everyone who loves is a
child of God and knows God, but the unloving know
nothing of God. For God is love; and his love was disclosed
to us in this, that he sent his only son into the world to bring
us life.' (1 John 4·7–9)
When Leonard Wilson eventually returned to England

from Singapore, he became Dean of Manchester and then, for sixteen years, Bishop of Birmingham. He had a full and a rich ministry; but it is doubtful whether it was ever fuller, or richer, than in those dark hours when he lay strapped to a table in the Secret Police Headquarters in the YMCA building in Singapore City and confessed, into the very faces of his tormentors, that Christ was Lord.

Another 'White Martyr', of an entirely different sort, and in entirely different circumstances, was meanwhile approaching his destiny far away in Sweden – Raoul Wallenburg.

7
THE SAVIOUR ANGEL

This was the title given to RAOUL WALLENBURG, a Swedish diplomat, by one of the many Jews whom he saved from deportation and death in the Budapest of 1944. His own eventual fate remains unknown; but his name has become honoured world-wide.

'We were hungry, thirsty, and frightened all the time . . .', wrote a man who was thirteen in Budapest in 1944 and who is now Director General of the Israeli Broadcasting Authority. 'One morning' he went on, 'a group of Fascists came into the house and said all the able-bodied women must go with them. We knew what this meant. My mother kissed me and I cried and she cried. We knew we were parting for ever and she left me there, an orphan to all intents and purposes. Then, two or three hours later, to my amazement, my mother returned with the other women . . . my mother was there – she was alive, and she was hugging me and kissing me, and she said one word: "Wallenburg". I knew who she meant because Wallenburg was a legend among the Jews. In the complete and total hell in which we lived, there was a saviour angel somewhere, moving around.'

There was, indeed, in the unlikely guise of a Swedish diplomat, young, handsome, well born, of a distinguished Swedish family. What he was doing in Budapest in 1944, and why he was engaged, so far as he was able, in the rescue of Jews destined for the death camps, is a singularly moving story. Moreover, it is not necessarily ended yet. Wallenburg may even now be alive, an aged man still a prisoner of Soviet Russia, somewhere in one of their prisons or labour camps. No-one knows, many attempts have been made to find out.

All have been, to date, unsuccessful. But what lives on in the grateful memory of thousands whom he helped, is the legend of his gallantry and devotion.

Raoul Wallenburg, was a martyr to a great cause — that of mercy and righteousness. He is recognized as a 'righteous Gentile' officially by the Government of Israel, and there is a memorial to him in the Avenue of the Righteous, in the great memorial complex to victims of the holocaust on a hilltop outside Jerusalem. A tree in that Avenue bears a plaque, and on that plaque is the name of Wallenburg. A medal has also been made which, as in the case of other righteous Gentiles, bears the inscription from the Talmud: 'Whoever saves a single soul, is as if he had saved the whole world.'

The story of Raoul Wallenburg cannot be understood at all without going back into the circumstances which made his heroism possible. The basic circumstance was the Nazi determination to exterminate, so far as possible, the whole of the Jewish race in Europe and wherever they could lay their hands upon them. This was a racial decision, unique in its horror in world history, and focussed upon nothing less than a mass act of genocide. The persecution of the Jews, which has a long, long history, and which was carried out in almost every European country throughout the centuries, reached its most extreme point in that which began in the Germany of the nineteen-thirties. The Nuremburg Laws made an outcast of every Jew, man or woman, excluding them from all civil rights and making them targets of what was seen as legitimate persecution. Their properties confiscated, their lives threatened, their families banned from schools and universities and many occupations: they became the pariahs of National Socialist Germany and its dependencies. And when Nazi power extended to other lands, all Jews in these territories were subject to the same persecutions.

The outbreak of World War II made the situation of the Jews far worse. Wherever they were, in whatever conquered country, from Norway to Italy, from France to Poland to

Russia, they became subject not only to the Nuremburg Laws but, with the passing of time, to something infinitely more terrible. This was The Final Solution, according to which nothing less than the extermination of the whole of Jewry was planned. By the end of 1943 millions of Jews had been sent to the death camps, most of them situated in Poland, where an assembly line machinery of death had been devised. It was carried out with great efficiency, and the manner in which it worked makes one of the most astonishing as well as the most tragic and appalling stories in human history.

The Jews in any country were first identified and located. They were then, when the time came, gathered together, first in local holding centres, then in centres where they were congregated in massive numbers as, for instance, at Drancy in France. From there they were sent by train, in cattle trucks nailed up, and usually containing some eighty people, on the long journey into Poland to whichever camp had been chosen for them. There, on detraining, they were immediately sorted out into males and females, into those fit for slave labour and those fit only for immediate death. The fate of the latter was often more merciful than that of the former. Those chosen for death were taken to what they imagined were baths, and required to undress. After that it was quite a short walk up to the open doors of the gas chamber. When this was full, the doors would close, the gas would be introduced, and death would take them in a few minutes. There followed the mass cremation of the remains, and the assembly line was ready for the next batch. Some idea of the scale of this operation can be gained by the fact that, at the height of the attempt to exterminate Hungarian Jewry, with which operation Wallenburg was involved, some six trains a day, each containing 5,000 souls, were being dispatched.

This was the operation which was carried out all over Europe from almost the earliest days of the war until nearly the end. The Jews of Germany had already gone. They were followed by those of Holland, 120,000, of Greece, 60,000, of France, 65,000, of Czechoslovakia, 120,000, of Belgium 25,000, of Bulgaria 12,000, of Italy 10,000, of Rumania 75,000, of Norway 7,000, of Denmark 425, of Yugoslavia, 10,000, of Poland, which had had one of the largest Jewish communities, a prodigious number. Of all these countries, by 1944, only Hungary had not contributed its victims, chiefly owing to the attitude taken by Admiral Horthy, the Regent, and others of his government who were reluctant to hand over their Jews. But by the March of 1944 the fate of Hungary's Jews was decided, and plans were put in hand to destroy them as soon as possible, before the already advancing Soviet armies were able to reach Hungary.

In the story of Wallenburg two dramatically contrasted characters now enter the scene, vivid personifications of evil on the one hand and good on the other. The evil was personified by an SS Officer who had been summoned to a meeting in the Mauthausen Concentration Camp on 12 March 1944. This was Adolph Eichmann, a man already notable within the SS for his organizational powers which had been demonstrated in the efficient working of the department of which he was the head, and which was concerned entirely with the carrying out of The Final Solution. He had already made his name, even before that Solution was promulgated, in ridding Austria of its Jews in the late 1930s. But he was more than a supremely efficient administrator. He considered it his duty to lay his hands as he put it, on every last Jew, and every one, and they were few, who eluded him he regarded as a judgement upon himself. In his total devotion to this inhuman task he was a wholly evil figure. When, in the years after the War, he was abducted by Israeli agents from South America and put on trial in Jerusalem, even they were not willing to pollute their land with his ashes after his execution. They were taken out to sea and disposed of there.

Confronting this dark figure was Raoul Wallenburg. He came from a distinguished Swedish family, whose father, an

72

Officer in the Swedish Navy, had died just before his birth. But Raoul's paternal grandfather, Gustave Wallenburg, had been an Ambassador and took upon himself the task of seeing that Raoul was educated as a cultured man of the world. He travelled quite extensively, visiting the United States and South Africa and other countries in the years before the War. But there was always within him the feeling that he should be acting under challenge, facing up to some trial the nature of which he did not know. Perhaps there was a hint of what was to come in an incident in the winter of 1942 when, with his half-sister, Raoul went to see a film in Stockholm. It was called Pimpernel Smith, featured the well known actor of that time, Leslie Howard, and told the story of a man who had managed to outwit the Nazis by arranging the escape of some of their victims, after the manner of that Scarlet Pimpernel of history who had, in the famous novel by Baroness Orckzy been shown as doing that very thing in the days of the French Revolution. When they came out of the cinema Raoul said to his sister that, if ever the chance came, he would like to do something on similar lines. His wish was to be fulfilled.

By this time rumours of what was really happening in the concentration camps had begun to leak out, principally through the testimonies of some few who had escaped. Some governments became seriously concerned, and approaches were made to the International Red Cross. The governments of the United States, of Sweden and Switzerland and Spain and Portugal and others were all aroused. It was known that 800,000 Jews in Hungary were immediately at risk. Because of this various countries were asked to step up their diplomatic representation in Hungary in order both to see and report on the situation and also to save as many Jews as possible by whatever means were available. One of the countries which decided to act in this way was Sweden. One of the diplomats they chose to send was Raoul Wallenburg, then in his early twenties. He arrived in Budapest in the July of 1944 at a time when the destruction of Hungary's Jews had reached what seemed to be a climax. By that time 437,402 had been transported to the death camps. There remained some 230,000 in Budapest itself. The provinces had been cleared; now the capital remained for treatment. In this situation Wallenburg brought to bear very considerable influences upon both the Hungarian Fascist Authorities and the SS themselves. He had a distinguished physical presence; fair, handsome, always very well turned out. He made much, too, of the fact that he was there as representative of the Swedish Government and Crown and of the most influential neutral power in Europe. The people he was dealing with, as well he knew, desired some respectability in the eyes of the world, grotesque as that may seem. And since this imposing Swedish Diplomat seemed to emanate dignity, they were all the more open to be influenced by him, as he moved fearlessly about the capital to their various offices in his large car with the Swedish flag.

But he was also ingenious. The passports which he devised were very carefully designed by him personally and, because of their imposing appearance as documents, proved to be extremely valuable. Many a Jewish life was saved by the fact that an arrested person was able to produce one of these passports. Some of the other diplomatic missions in the city had, certainly, documents of their own; but none of them proved as effective as these. They also restored some sense of dignity to those Jews who were able to obtain them. Wallenburg also busied himself with the establishment of hospitals, nurseries, and feeding centres using funds made available to him by American Jewish organizations and others. Eventually he gathered around him a staff of several hundred Jews, and it was a measure of his extraordinary influence that he was able to exempt these people from the otherwise compulsory wearing of the yellow star. He himself worked untiringly, and always with immense personal courage. There was an occasion when he went to the station to intercept a transport already loaded with Jewish men and walked along the roof of the trucks handing in copies of his passport to the outstretched hands of prisoners, all the time in full view of an armed guard on the platform. He then claimed that all those who possessed these things should in fact be released and, such was his extraordinary influence, this was actually done.

A man who, as a leading member of the Central Jewish Council, encountered both Wallenburg and Eichmann at this time left a vivid recollection of how the two men struck him. His memory highlights the impression that in the confrontation of these two men there was indeed an element of darkness encountering the light. Eichmann, he recorded, was 'a born, inveterate criminal to whom other beings' pain was lust. In moments of sincerity he called himself a bloodhound.' Wallenburg, on the other hand, was 'unselfish, full of endless élan and the will to work. Like all truly great men his example induced the other neutral legations to emulate him and join in the struggle.' Wallenburg, in a letter to a friend at this time spoke of his activities in characteristically modest words. 'When I now look back on the three months I have spent here I can only say that it has been a most interesting experience and, I believe, not without results. . . . It has been my object all the time to try to help all Jews.'

But some of the memories which have survived of his gallant and selfless activities paint a picture in much stronger colours. There was a girl, seventeen at the time, who was involved in one of the so-called death marches of Jewish women which were imposed upon them when rail transport had become difficult. They were required to walk to the Hungarian frontier and all the way onwards to their deaths. This girl, recalling it all in her old age, remembered the cold, the rain, and the brutality. She remembered lying on the ground at night in several degrees of frost. When her convoy reached the point where trains were to take them the last stages, she was desperately ill, lying semi-conscious on the ground. She was aroused by hearing a cry from the women around: 'Wallenburg! And then she saw him: clean, smart, even elegant in his fur hat. How he managed it this woman never realized; but those to whom he was able to distribute some of his certificates were eventually sent back to Budapest.

As the momentum of the persecution increased, Wallenburg was to be seen often, distinguished by his leather coat and fur cap, arguing and protesting face to face with SS and Hungarian Officers, usually with some terror-struck crowd of Jews in the background. He was always ready to put his own life on the line. Once, when a round up of Jewish men was in progress Wallenburg told the officer in charge that if he went ahead with the arrests he would find that it was necessary to shoot him, Wallenburg, first.

There was an occasion, when an attempt had been made on his life, that Wallenburg, knowing that this had been instigated by Eichmann, walked into the latter's headquarters and protested. The SS Officer apologized, an unheard of happening. Shortly after this Wallenburg invited Eichmann to dinner and there, in an elegant house which had been taken over from a rich Jewish family, the two men, darkness and light personified, discussed with frigid mutual politeness, their totally different viewpoints. They parted, never to meet again, Eichmann going to his eventual death at the hands of the Jews whom he had persecuted, Wallenburg to an end the nature of which remains to this day unknown.

He remained behind in Budapest after other Diplomatic Missions had withdrawn. His purpose was to further the liberation of remaining Jews and to help them to some kind of rehabilitation. When Soviet Forces eventually reached the city he sought out the first detachment he could find and requested that he should be taken to Army Headquarters. There he was able to meet the Army Commander who gave him a pass onwards to higher military authority. What happened precisely after that is not known. Meanwhile, the Russians had discovered in the two surviving ghettos in Budapest some 100,000 Jews still surviving. The great majority of these, it has been estimated, owed their lives to Raoul Wallenburg. Those whom he had saved expressed

76

their gratitude in moving terms. We 'solemnly commem-morate your immortal achievement and heroic fight' said one testimony in 1945 forwarded to the Swedish Foreign Office. This was at a time when no one knew where he was, just as no one has known since. Evidence exists that he was encountered in various Moscow prisons in the late forties and early fifties. Subsequently, over the years, other reports have filtered through although, after a long time denying that he was in their hands, the Russians claimed that he had in fact died of a heart attack while in prison in Moscow in 1947. But it seems clear that he has been seen in later years, still a prisoner. And there, it seems, his tale must end.

But not quite. He has left behind him an inspiring legend and an example of selfless sacrifice which shines still as a light in a dark world. Gideon Hausmer, Prosecutor of Eichmann, said of Wallenburg that 'He won his battle and I feel that in this age when there is little to believe in – so very little on which our young people can pin their hopes and ideals – he is a person to show to the world, which knows so little about him. That is why I believe the story of Raoul Wallenburg should be told and his figure, in all its true proportions, projected into human minds.'

His inclusion in any gallery of Christian Martyrs, of this or any other century, should need no justification. He can stand among those who have confessed Christ, and him crucified, not because of anything which he may have said or claimed; but on grounds of a great love which led him to lay down his life for those whom he saw as his friends – the persecuted, the lost whom he sought out and found. Another, and a greater, did that before him, and it was surely in the pattern of Christ that Wallenburg's sacrifice is to be seen. 'If you know that he is righteous' wrote St John, speaking of this Christ, 'you must recognize that every man who does right is his child.' (1 John 2:29.) And that, surely, can be said of Wallenburg. He could have enjoyed a rich and fortunate life: he chose, quite voluntarily, a harder path. And if a martyr is one who undergoes suffering for a great cause, then surely his place is among them. The haunting possibility remains that he is still alive, a very old man in some Soviet prison. The last report of him was that he was in the Leningrad area prison hospital in 1980. Before that there were reports of sightings, or rumours of his presence in the Lubianka prison, Moscow, 1951; the Vladimir prison, 1951, the Gorki Transit prison, 1955, a mental institution in Moscow, 1961, the isolation barracks, Wrangel Island, in the Arctic Ocean, 1962, and several others. In any event he lives still in the hearts and minds of many people, and perhaps in their consciences also. There was an exhibition of his story in the crypt of St Martins in the Fields church, London in 1982.

Included in the booklet about Wallenburg in that exhibition was a striking poem about him which began

> Does no one heed me
> Tapping on the wall
> Talking to yesterday's ghosts?
> Do I exist only
> In my old tired, tortured mind?

Another most gifted man, whose death is a certainty, was at this same time in prison in Germany.

8

THE VOICE FROM PRISON

It is a sorrowful thought that the German theologian DIETRICH BONHOEFFER could have made a notable contribution to Christian thinking in the years since the Second World War. His gifts would have been needed. But it was not to be. And yet, strangely enough 'he being dead yet speaketh', and the story of his martyrdom continues to move many.

'It is a miracle of the years that follow that in fact the Christian faith did break through . . ., and that there was no lack of men and women, both in the Catholic and in the Protestant churches of Germany, who were ready for the sake of their faith to risk all that they had, not excluding their lives, when individual acts of splended courage showed that the church of the Apostles and the Martyrs was not dead.' So wrote Mary Bosanquet in her life of the great German theologian and eventual martyr, Dietrich Bonhoeffer. By 'the years that followed', she is referring to that period in Germany which saw the struggle of conscience of many Germans following the rise of Hitler and the events which led up to the war. Among the 'individual acts of splendid courage' which did show the true life of the church, few can have been greater than that which eventually took Bonhoeffer to his martyr's death.

But his is not a simple story: he was not a simple man; but a highly intellectual individual, brought up in a cultured German family. His father was Professor of Psychiatry and Director of the University Hospital for nervous diseases in Breslau. Dietrich, the future martyr, was the youngest of a family of six. He had a happy childhood; but his decision to study theology at University brought concern to his family. It was not in their tradition. For the most part, the family was scientific, although the mother had a deep strain of christian piety. There were many arguments; but always the young Dietrich held out, utterly convinced of the reality of God. He used to say that, whatever they did to him, he would still go on believing. It was a curious premonition of what was to come in the time ahead when far greater pressures were to be brought upon him to abandon a God whom it seemed had abandoned him. As a student in the early twenties he was an imposing figure, over six foot, broad and strong, with blue eyes and strong features beneath curly fair hair.

In this period the young Dietrich encountered the full impact of a church other than his own when he visited Rome. He had never before seen anything like the splendours which were there revealed to him; the devotions of the people in Easter week, the crowded confessionals, the processions, the music. Hitherto his experiences of the church had been confined to the studies of the theologians and the not very inspiring life of the provincial confessional church in Germany. Now here was a new thing altogether. But this did not move him in any way to desert the church of his own traditions; but rather to see in both Catholic and Protestant a great unified truth which it was to be his concern always to maintain. He said: 'We repeat the same Creed, we pray the same Our Father, and we have many customs in common. That unites us, and as far as we are concerned we will gladly live in peace beside this unequal sister. We are not concerned with the name Catholic or Protestant, but with the word of God.'

This vision of the church in its widest sense, invested with the power of the word and with tradition and with the devotions of generations of Christian people continued to inspire him as the international skies darkened over Germany. Shortly after his ordination he was sent to work in a German congregation in Spain. There, in 1928, in one of his earliest sermons he made one of his most striking confessions of faith. 'There is only one hope for our age, which is so powerless, so feeble, so wretched, disliked and pitiable, and with all this so forlorn a return to the church, to the place where one man bears up another in love, where one man shares a life of another, where there is fellowship in God, where there is home, where there is love. . . .'

One other passage from these early sermons strikes home still, and gives a vivid impression of the sincerity with which Bonhoeffer looked upon all things sacred. 'Blessed are the pure in heart, for they shall see God', he began. And he went on: 'As in ancient Israel any man who touched the Ark of the Covenant forfeited his life, because a divine power went forth from it against which he could not stand. So likewise the man who approaches too near to the word of our text today, must lose his life before him. Such wonderful powers go forth from it, it shines with such wondrous and quiet radiance, that we cannot turn our eyes away. . . . So I bring you today this word in my text, and I know that the best thing we can do with the face of it is to be silent. To gaze and be silent, to let the word pierce us and master us, to loose our life to this word and to let it lift us into eternal heights and distances.'

Meanwhile, in the private and inner life of Bonhoeffer many things were developing. He had received his doctorate of theology. At the same time, in his public life in the Germany of his day, he was conscious, as were so many others, of clouds over the whole national scene. The Weimar republic was manifestly failing. A huge inflation had signified an economic collapse, and the rise of extremist political parties was another sign of the bad times ahead. It was a time of dread for all those who sought to hold on to democratic ideals. It was a time also of much disturbance of conscience for those who saw the increasing injustices of their society, including growing persecution of the Jews. Bonhoeffer wrote of this time: 'the avenging Lord before

81

whom we bow is also the Lord of promise. He alone knows his people, he is here, perhaps in the midst of us. He alone knows to whom he is speaking when he says, "to him that overcometh will I give to eat of the tree of life, which is in the midst of the paradise of God". Will this be ourselves, shall we overcome, shall we have faith to the end? The future makes us afraid, but the promise comforts us. Blessed are those to whom it is spoken.' He could scarcely have known how extraordinarily prophetic of his own fate these words were to be.

Hitler came to power on the 30 January 1933. If there was any historical moment when Germany entered the dark tunnel of her impending destiny, then this was it. Bonhoeffer had by this time developed extensive contacts in the United States, where he had visited more than once. He had also visited Britain, made even more contacts, and was beginning to spend time there. But in Germany itself there was much to challenge a Christian; pressures to support the Nazi power; the growing persecution of the Jews. The essence of the struggle in which Bonhoeffer found himself involved was, apart from those aspects of political and racial tyranny, one which was basically a struggle of the church to preserve its own freedom to instruct its youth. There were many agonizing questions to be faced. There were, to take one instance alone, the tensions which were bound to arise between the patriotism of a German at a time when National Socialism was bringing something of a national revival. The church was infected, and it was no small thing to oppose the tide of popular acclaim of all that Nazism was thought to be achieving. It was also dangerous. From this time onwards Bonhoeffer, with many others, became a marked man.

There was also in his life another tension something which arose, and which increased as the years went by and the general scene darkened: that God did not seem a necessity to much of humanity. When, in due time, Bonhoeffer came to be criticized for the development of the idea of 'religionless Christianity', it was this issue which lay at the heart of the matter. The events through which he was living brought him face to face with what he felt to be the need of a new expression of the Christian faith which would enable it to speak with power to the secular world. How, if he had lived, he would have worked to put this concept forward, is a fascinating thought.

The coming of war changed everything. All those tensions which had been building up inside Germany were now intensified. The penalties for opposition became more severe. For those who saw in the rise of Hitler not only the destruction of the Germany they had loved, but also a denial of christian values, life became perilous. As it happened, Bonhoeffer was in America when war came. He could have remained there. But he chose to return, and because of this decision he was to die. He became involved in the plot, in which many of the finest Germans were concerned, to kill Hitler.

But so stark a statement does less than justice to Bonhoeffer as a Christian. The larger truth is that he had become convinced of the increasing evil of the regime. He had made contacts with fellow Christians in allied countries, in whom he placed hopes for the liberation of Germany. What became known as 'the July Plot', the attempt to assassinate Hitler in the July of 1944, had been long in preparation, and had engaged the energies, and was to cost the lives of many fine men and women.

When Bonhoeffer was in Geneva at the outset of the war he was asked what it was which he prayed for in those times. He replied; 'If you want to know the truth, I pray for the defeat of my nation, for I believe that that is the only way to pay for all the suffering which my country has caused in the world.' Later he said, 'If we claim to be Christians there is no room for expediency. Hitler is anti-Christ; we must go on with our work and eliminate him, whether he be successful or not.'

Among Bonhoeffer's friends in allied countries was Bishop Bell of Chichester. This far-seeing man, had he been listened to, might have developed bonds with Christians in Germany which, by shortening the war, could have avoided the suffering of its later years. As early as 1942, Bonhoeffer was writing to Bell, whom he had met in neutral Sweden, in affectionate terms. 'Let me express my deep and sincere gratitude for the hours you have spent with me. It still seems to me like a dream to have seen you, to have spoken to you, to have heard your voice. I think these days will remain in my memory as some of the greatest in my life. This spirit of fellowship and Christian brotherhood will carry me through the darkest hour, and even if things go worse than we hope and expect the light of these few days will never be extinguished in my heart. God be with you on your way home, in your work, and always. Please pray for us. We need it.'

Bonhoeffer's involvement in the July plot took him close to the inner counsels of some in the military circles of Germany, where members of the high commands were implicated. Among such persons was Admiral Canaris, the discovery of whose diary had tragic consequences. There were several attempts upon Hitler's life. All failed. Finally, in the July of 1944, a distinguished officer, Klaus von Staufenburg, placed a bomb under the conference table in Hitler's Headquarters in the east. This time the device did explode. But Hitler, although wounded, survived. Meanwhile the plotters, assuming the success of the plan, had passed the word that take-over operations in Berlin and elsewhere should go ahead as agreed. It was too late to cancel these orders. The plot was revealed, and a massive action went into operation to arrest those involved.

Bonhoeffer had already been in prison some time, arrested on suspicion, and had served some two years before the end came. His arrest had been the beginning of his tribulations. He described in one of his letters what happened when he was taken to the Tegel military prison in Berlin. 'The formalities of admission were correctly completed. For the first night I was locked up in an admission cell. The blankets on the camp bed had such a foul smell that in spite of the cold it was impossible to use them. Next morning a piece of bread was thrown into my cell; I had to pick it up from the floor. The sound of vile abuse of the prisoners who were held for investigation penetrated into my cell for the first time; since then I have heard it every day, from morning to night.'

It was from this prison that Bonhoeffer sent his *Letters From Prison*, which have become a twentieth century classic. With extraordinary powers of concentration he was able, even in those circumstances, to think through some of the problems of faith which had been with him all his life. Chiefly in these letters his concept of 'the world coming of age' was worked out. It has been greatly misunderstood. In essence, his concern was with how God could be made to matter to in a non religious world. In some respects, he came to believe, the church had ceased to have the right to speak and would continue not to have that right until it had recovered its soul. 'Our being Christians today,' he wrote, 'will be limited to two things, prayer, and righteous action among men. All Christian thinking, speaking, and organizing must be born anew out of this prayer and action.' In a 'World come of age', men must learn to act as grown up sons of God, rather than as undeveloped children of God, and to be responsible for their own actions.

The scene darkened for Bonhoeffer and for others of his friends when they were moved, in the October of the first year of his imprisonment, to the Gestapo prison in the Prinz Albrecht Strasse. The war was now closing in on Berlin. In this the February of 1945 Bonhoeffer, in company with other 'special prisoners', was sent south towards the concentration camp at Buchenwald.

But for one chance happening the world might never have come to know what Bonhoeffer was like in those final days of his life, nor how his character and his soul had developed. As it happened, a certain Captain Payne Best, a British officer who had been captured in 1940, was transferred to Buchenwald shortly after Bonhoeffer's arrival there, and was with him during his last weeks. The value of his testimony is increased by the fact that he had no previous knowledge of Bonhoeffer. He was profoundly impressed. 'Bonhoeffer', he wrote, 'was different; just quite calm and normal, seemingly perfectly at his ease yet his soul really shone in the dark desperation of our prison.'

Bonhoeffer's spiritual struggle had led at last to the complete abandonment of self. His brilliance, the great promise which he knew would lie in a future if only he could reach it, were all put aside. He turned to the cross and to Christ and, in a mysterious way, was, it seems, absorbed in it. He was, Payne Best wrote, 'all humility and sweetness. He always seemed to diffuse an atmosphere of happiness, a joy in every smallest event of life, and a deep gratitude for the mere fact that he was alive. . . . He was one of the very few men I have ever met to whom his God was real and ever close to him.'

The Easter of 1945 was now approaching. The 'special prisoners' were kept to themselves at Buchenwald. But early in April special orders were received from Berlin; they were to be taken on to another camp at Flossenburg. So they were driven on down the narrow corridor which was all that was left of German territory. They reached Regensburg and from there, along refugee crowded roads, they moved to the village of Schonberg. Spirits were high; the party was increasingly sure that their deliverance was near. But they were wrong. That fatal diary of Admiral Canaris had been found. An official was dispatched from Berlin with orders for the execution of Canaris himself and five others, including Bonhoeffer.

On the Sunday after Easter his companions asked him to hold a service in the school house where they were held. He was hesitant; most of those with him were Catholics and there was also a prisoner from communist Russia. But it was this man in particular who pressed for the service. Bonhoeffer spoke to the text; 'Through his stripes we are healed.' (Isa. 53:5), and 'Blessed be the God and Father of our

Lord Jesus Christ, which according to his abundant mercy has begotton us again into a live hope by the resurrection of Jesus Christ from the dead' (1 Pet. 1:3). Captain Payne Best wrote later of this time that Bonhoeffer 'reached the hearts of all, finding just the right words to express the spirit of our imprisonment, and the thoughts and resolutions it had brought.'

Then, just as the service had ended, the door of the school house was thrown open. Two men stood there. One of them gave a command; 'Prisoner Bonhoeffer, come with us.' Everyone recognized the phrase; it meant death. So Bonhoeffer turned to go, speaking as he went to Payne Best, asking him to take a message to Bishop Bell in England. The words he used are unforgettable. 'Tell him,' he said, 'that for me this is the end; but also the beginning. . . .' He was taken back to Flossenburg, and interrogated through the night. Just before dawn, together with Admiral Canaris, and two others, he was brought from his cell to hear sentence read. Present was a prison doctor who, years later, remembered that 'through a half open door in one of the huts I saw Pastor Bonhoeffer, still in his prison clothes, kneeling in fervent prayer to the Lord his God. The devotion and evident conviction of being heard that I saw in the prayer of this intensely captivating man moved me to the depths.'

Soon afterwards, naked in the dawn, Bonhoeffer was hanged.

9
KIKUYU HERO

Among the many names recorded in the Book of Martyrs an exceptional number are those of members of the Kikuyu people of Kenya. All died for their Christian faith at the hands of Mau Mau terrorists. One of them was ANDREW KAGURU, a farm worker.

In his book *So Rough a Wind,* Sir Michael Blundell tells of the struggle for independence in Kenya marked by the war against the Mau Mau. As a distinguished figure in the Kenya of his day, Sir Michael picks out two elements on the African side of the conflict. There were those who believed that advance was best achieved by close co-operation with the Government in order to embrace knowledge and learn the white man's abilities as quickly as possible as a step on the road to independence, and those who thought that subversion and acts of violence would best free them from the rule of the European. Both sides had the same aim: the independence of the Kikuyu people from British rule. He then goes on to mark a third element in the situation, the many firm and devout Christians among the members of the Kikuyu Tribe who ranged themselves with those who believed that independence could best come by peaceful means. He wrote: 'It was these men who banded together and resisted with the greatest heroism and courage the terrible physical atrocities and debasing of the human mind which Mau Mau attempted to inflict upon the Kikuyu people. Many were tortured and killed in the process, but eventually it was these men and women, with the adherents which they were able to attract, who broke the force of Mau Mau and the terrorist gangs.'

Notable among these devout Christians, and included in

the long list of Kikuyu martyrs, was a farm worker called Andrew Kaguru. He died for his Christian faith. But how that destiny came upon him, how it befell that this simple man had to die – cut to pieces with pangas, the favourite weapon of the Mau Mau – cannot be understood unless his story is seen in the context of what was happening in Kenya in the early nineteen fifties.

The modern face of that country, until somewhat marred by the revolt of some service personnel in the later summer of 1982, was one of prosperity and tranquility for many years under the rule of Jomo Kenyatta. Unique in this respect among the newly independent States of modern Africa, it seemed, as it still does, one of the few in which African and European, black and white, the new masters and the old, could live together in accord. But it can easily be forgotten, as the years roll by, how terrible was the inception of this prosperous country, and how bitter was the struggle which was one of the factors in bringing it about.

The country was very much the creation of the white settler who, often from a somewhat aristocratic British background, came to farm in this beautiful country. This development began in the late nineteenth century when Joseph Thomson made the first journey to Uganda through what was to become the cultivated settled area of Kenya. Then in 1902 came the Uganda Railway with the development of the land alongside it inspired by the enthusiasm of Sir Charles Elliot, Commissioner of what was then known as British East Africa. The society which eventually emerged was paternalistic as regards the native peoples, into whose great spaces these white Europeans had come and created the handsome farms. Notable, in fact predominant, among these native peoples was the great tribe of the Kikuyu described by Sir Michael as 'an extremely intelligent and industrious people, with a great ability and a natural acquisitiveness. In the tight Colonial world of those days they must have suffered much from the inferior position which was imposed upon them. I have often thought how patiently some of them accepted the stupidities and the little arrogances which I regret a few of us used in our dealings with them.' Yet, on the whole, relations between the British and the native peoples were close and often affectionate. The situation changed with the rise of national consciousness among the Africans and, in Kenya, notably among the Kikuyu. As they increasingly absorbed a European outlook, so increasingly they came to see the justice of their cause. It was a cause embittered by land hunger, especially in the rural areas.

The rise of Mau Mau was a savage phenomenon, and the war which resulted a savage war. Various attempts have been made to explain the title of this secret society, or movement, perhaps the nearest to it is that it was a shortened form for 'Mzunga Aenda Ulaya Mwaafrike Apate Uhuru', which in the Kiswahili language of East Africa means 'White man go to Europe so the African may gain independence.' And that concisely sums up the purposes of the movement. It was organized on a cell system. There were gangs in the forest or on the farms with off-shoots in villages and towns who provided Mau Mau terrorists with recruits, food, weapons and all that they needed as far as possible. Basic to membership of a Mau Mau gang was the taking of an oath binding those involved to absolute obedience to Mau Mau commands. These oaths, frequently obscene in ritual, were extremely powerful. The story was told of an old man on a farm, who had worked there for forty years, who yet urged his master to shut him out of the house at dusk because otherwise, he said, he would be forced to kill him.

There were, in the early fifties, a whole series of ghastly murders. The attacks came mostly in the early evening while the doors at the back of a farmhouse were still open and the owners would not be suspicious of a servant entering a room. Then a gang would rush in and the victims would be slashed to death, irrespective of sex or age. A horrid example of such killings was the murder of Mr and Mrs Ruck, a young couple, with their son Michael, who were butchered in their own home. Yet Mrs Ruck was a doctor well known for her work among the Kikuyu, whom she had helped freely and generously. Even worse was what became known as the Lari Massacre, in the March of 1953, when Mau Mau killed Kikuyu families and women and children wholesale.

Inevitably, it was the murders of white settlers which, internationally, made the headlines. But the fate of many of the Kikuyu themselves, those of them who would not take the Mau Mau oath, or assist the terrorists, was far worse and on a larger scale. Hundreds of them perished violently. Thousands of them for a long time lived in dread. Those who lived in the countryside, employed upon white-owned farms, were particularly vulnerable. Living, according to custom, on the farm estate in their own hut, together with others all surrounded by a fence and called a Shamba, they had little protection against gangs who could come upon them at night. It required very great heroism to sustain opposition to Mau Mau in such circumstances, and this is the point at which the story of Andrew Kaguru comes into focus.

He was a Kikuyu Christian. The faith had come to his people in the early years of this century, so that he was among the first generation of those affected by it. It would be wrong to use the word 'conversion'; because there was no experience of that kind in Andrew's life. It was as though he came to full acceptance of the implications of it, in terms of faithfulness and loyalty, only gradually and slowly, which is something, after all, characteristic of the countryman in all ages and places. But he went to a Mission School, one which had been opened by an early missionary to the Kikuyu. He was still only a boy, and a very typical lively and mischievous one as well, when he first went to work on a farm.

The owner of this was called Frank Watkins; but his African workers called him Gateru which means 'man with a beard'. Here Andrew lived on a Shamba with his mother and sister where he worked at first tending a flock of turkeys kept by his employer's wife.

Before long a school and a church were built nearby, and by Africans. When the school was completed, in the building of which his employer had helped, Andrew attended it. At the same time he began to go to church and, when he asked for baptism, was given the name Andrew. He was certainly no saint at this time, by any means. As a boy he had been mischievous and quarrelsome: now, as a man, he was also quite often drunk. He had married a girl, Alice, who herself was a nominal Christian although she had been baptized, just as her new husband had been. But soon a moral challenge came to Andrew Kaguru, as though it were some kind of preparation for the immense spiritual one which was to come upon them.

His master Gateru, the man with a beard, died, so Andrew and his wife had to move elsewhere for work. They went to the farm owned by a daughter of their former employer, a Mrs Hill. Not long after their first going there, she fell ill and was taken away to hospital, leaving Andrew in charge. Her friends warned her that this was a risky thing to do, since it was quite possible that he would make off with everything. It would have been better, friends told her, to have left a European in charge of the place. But Andrew did not behave in that way at all. He could not have been more trustworthy or faithful; regularly he would cycle in to the hospital to report progress to Mrs Hill. Obviously, a change had taken place in him of a very deep kind, and that was true. He had been deeply affected by a sermon at his village church. The essence of the message he heard was that God is holy, knows the secrets of mens' hearts, and grieves for mens' sins. It seemed a simple message; but the results of it in Andrew were profound. When Mrs Hill, selling her farm, offered to help him find another post, he declined, saying that he had resolved to return home and devote himself to doing what he now saw was the Lord's work among his own people.

This was an extraordinary change. Back in his native area, he worked for five years as a pastor, teaching in the school,

93

visiting people in their homes, urging those who had been nominal Christians to become real Christians.

Thus the scene was set for the spiritual challenge in the life of Andrew Kaguru which followed the moral challenge of years before. The Mau Mau were now at the peak of their activities, and the taking of the oath loomed large in their campaign. For their purposes it was of the utmost importance that all Africans should do this, since the more who abstained, so much the more was their purpose weakened. Very great pressures were therefore made upon all Kikuyu to take the oath, and extreme measures were followed to frighten those who did not. Many refusers were murdered in the presence of crowds of natives forcibly gathered together to witness the happening. On the other hand, there were many Christians who openly encouraged their fellows in the faith, and among this number was Andrew. For him, as for others, this dissident action was a duty arising from faith. After all, they had been taught by that faith to swear no oaths, and this principle they maintained to the death. The quality of the Kikuyu martyrs – and there were many of them besides Andrew Kaguru, just as heroic, just as constant – cannot be properly appreciated without realizing that they were not in any sense instruments of the white man, supporting his rule against the wishes of their own people, so much as brave contenders against a tyranny given added terror by the operation of their pagan oath.

It was never possible to know who had taken this oath and who had not. Clearly, there were some in the congregation to whom Andrew ministered at this time who had. These reported him to Mau Mau leaders in the forest, and it was from these that a party of armed men was sent, at dead of night, to break into his hut. He was at once seized. Alice, his wife, was forced to look upon him as he stood there in the grip of his captors. One of them asked her:

'Will you take the oath, or we will kill your husband?'

'Never', she replied. 'I am a Christian.'

'We will save you, if you will.'

'We will never do it', Andrew said, 'so what you are going to do, do quickly.'

Alice was then symbolically cut with the panga blades, although not fatally, and became unconscious as she was thrown to the floor. She was still unconscious when Andrew was taken outside and cut to pieces.

That brief dialogue in the hut of Andrew Kaguru was quoted earlier in the introduction to this book, as an instance of how extraordinarily similar it was, in form and content, to a Christian martyrdom in the ancient world when, in much the same way, a person was challenged to take an oath and threatened with death if they refused. It seems that this is a constant threat running through the great tapestry of martyrdom; the refusal to do something deeply felt to be a betrayal of the faith even at the price of life itself. What went through the mind of Andrew, that Kikuyu farm worker, in the last moments of his life when he was faced with a horrible end? Some power greater than himself by far must have come upon him, and inspired him, and upheld him. It is a great mystery, and one can only look upon it in humility. It is also a challenge – the challenge which all the martyrs present, of wondering whether we ourselves would be capable of such courage, constancy, and faithfulness.

The Archbishop of Canterbury in those years, Geoffrey Fisher, visited Kenya at about this time for the inauguration of a new self-governing province for Central Africa. Recalling this occasion, he said to the writer of these words: 'That, indeed, was memorable. The Mau Mau business was still going on; and I was to lay the foundation stone of a new church to be built in memory of the African martyrs at the hands of the Mau Mau. When robed, we went in procession through Askaris lining the route, down to the place where the foundation stone was to be laid. We had a canopy over us to keep possible rain off, there was an oblong space roped off, and round it a mass of African Christians of the Diocese of Fort Hall, each with a little board in front of him saying the mission from which they came. They were all on the level, but from them the ground rose steeply, and this rising ground was crammed with Africans. I said, "Who are these?" And they said, "They are gate-crashers from all the districts around, probably Mau Mau to a man. They must all have taken the first oath."'

The foundation stone which the Archbishop laid was to become the Cathedral at Fort Hall, built to commemorate more than 1,500 Kikuyu martyrs, including Andrew Kaguru.

Another man – young, white, and American – two years later in the United States, endured a martyr's death in very different circumstances.

10
YOUNG MAN WITH A CAUSE

The struggle for Civil Rights for the black people of the American South has been a classic twentieth century conflict, involving passion on both sides, disturbing the conscience of the United States itself, and claiming lives. One of these lives was that of JONATHAN DANIELS, a young Episcopal Church seminarian, shot in Haynesville, Alabama, in 1965.

Civil Rights in the United States in the fifties and sixties was a cause which caught at the consciences, and moved the hearts of all sorts and conditions of people, like that Mrs Liuzzo the housewife who was shot in her car between Montgomery and Selma, Alabama. But, apart from Martin Luther King, few names caught the headlines internationally, and though their deaths made impact in the United States itself, comparatively few were heard of elsewhere. The case of Jonathan Daniels, a young seminarian who met his death by a shot gun blast on 20 August 1965 illustrates the point. His name is in the Book of Martyrs in Canterbury Cathedral; but it is not one widely known, for all that. Yet his was a true martyr's death, in as much as he was prepared to go to the limit for the cause he supported, and because of the Christian faith which moved him to embrace that cause and die for it. His story is all the more worth telling because it picks out in some detail what it was really like to be involved in the Civil Rights Movement, how sharp was the challenge it presented, and how ugly were the prejudices and how brutal their expression which surrounded the whole matter.

When Jonathan Daniels had gone down to Selma to join in the protests there, he was one day queueing at the counter of the Post Office when the man in front of him turned round, looked at his clerical collar and at the badge he was wearing, and then announced: 'Know what he is? He is a white nigger'. When Jonathan wrote about this incident in the Journal of his Theological College, he added: 'I was not happy thus to become the object of every gaze. And yet deep within me rose an affirmation and a tenderness and a joy that wanted to shout. Yes! If pride were appropriate in the ambiguities of my presence in Selma, I should be unspeakably proud of my title. As I type now, my hands are hopelessly white. But my heart is black.'

During this same time in Selma Jonathan joined the congregation of St Pauls Episcopal Church in that town, which was an all white congregation and wished at that time to remain so. The difficulty, from the church's point of view, was that when Jonathan went there for service he took with him a number of young blacks. They were allowed in; but in the back pew. During the week, when Jonathan was sitting in his car at a traffic light, he was accosted by a man who got out of his own car and came over. He asked: 'Are you the scum that's been going to the Episcopal Church? That's what you are – you and the nigger trash you bring with you.' Yet people like this man were decent citizens, as they saw it and, moreover, they had to live in Selma in a tense Black–White situation which had been going on for years. People like Daniels were, in their eyes, outsiders making, as they saw it, a bad situation worse.

Martin Luther King had appealed for volunteers from the North to go down and help out in Selma at the height of the Civil Rights Campaign. Many answered that appeal, and it was an invitation in his college to contribute to the expenses of someone who, connected with the place, was in fact going South, that moved Jonathan to wonder whether he should go himself. At once, like the man in the Gospel story, and like no doubt, many others would in a similar situation, he 'began to make excuses'. He was busy; he had his studies to work at. But he would at least contribute, and so he put his money in the envelope provided. But somehow this did not seem adequate and that evening, in the college chapel, during the singing of the Magnificat, at the words: 'He has showed strength with his arm: He has scattered the proud in the imagination of their hearts. He has put down the mighty from their seat, and has exalted the humble and meek', he knew that it wasn't enough. And so he took a plane and went himself, first for a stay of nine days, and then, by permission of his college, for a long stay as an official representative of his Church's Society for Cultural and Racial Unity. He lived with a Negro family.

No one could have guessed that in just over six months he was to meet his death.

He was very young when that happened. Born in 1939 in the New Hampshire town of Keene, he was the son of a well-known physician, and of Constance Daniels, his wife, a former teacher. Writing later, when Jonathan was entering Theological College, he testified to the influence for good his father had been, especially through his example of sacrificial service of his patients. In spite of this happy home background, Jonathan had himself passed through the usual tumultuous adolescent years, being for a time very rebellious and wild. Then that phase passed, and he became again his own warm self. But in one respect he did not return to what he had been as a boy. Many people, in the process of growing up, abandon the religious beliefs of childhood; but in Jonathan's case this turning away was rather more radical. By the time he came to graduate from the Virginia Military Institute in Lexington, Virginia, he had become very much a free thinker, turning aside, except for nominal attendances, from the church of which, at any rate back home in Keene, he had been at one time an enthusiastic member. But he had left his college with some distinction and this enabled him to enrol in the Harvard Graduate School in 1961. In the Easter of the following year, when he attended a

Communion Service in the Church of the Advent in Boston, he underwent a religious experience – he called it a 'reconversion' – which, proving lasting, had profound effects upon such life as was left to him.

Conversion can take many forms, and affect many people in different ways. In some, it is so gradual as scarcely to be perceptible: only a slow growing in faith and understanding and love of Christ over the years. But with others it can be a genuine 'Damascus Road' experience – sudden and dramatic – and this appears to have been the case with Jonathan. Maybe it was the kind of reaction which was in tune with his particular kind of personality. Some of his letters seem to speak of an emotional personality. When he was living with the Negro family in Selma he could be moved to tears by the thought that a small child in the family did not love him as he had expected her to do, and equally delighted when it eventually emerged that she did. Then, as he put it, 'I knew something very important and incredibly beautiful had happened.' And later, when he was on the verge of entering upon his theological training he wrote of himself: 'My strengths are intelligence, sensitivity, conscientiousness, honesty, introspection, critical perception. . . . I am quick to see a need and anxious to help. My weaknesses are insecurity and consequent lack of initiative, excessive concern for external opinion, frequent and almost paralysing doubt, perfectionism and procrastination.' What comes through seems to be an emotional, generous-hearted, impulsive character capable, as events were to show, of superb courage.

The outcome of the experience at the communion service in Boston's Church of the Advent was that henceforth Jonathan felt himself committed to Christ. Thus it came about that after a year at home in Keene, New Hampshire, during which he filled various jobs, he was accepted by his Bishop as a candidate for the Ministry and entered the Episcopal Theological School in Cambridge Massachusetts. While a student there made the decision to respond to

Luther King's appeal and, with many others from the North, to go down to Selma.

During his first stay there he was busy furthering, as far as possible, the Negro cause among the white population, especially Episcopalians, members of his own Church in the town. It was hard and thankless work, not often productive of apparent gain. He wrote at this time 'This is the stuff with which our life is made. There are moments of great joy and moments of sorrow. Almost imperceptibly some men grow in grace. Some men don't. Christian hope, grounded in the reality of Easter, must never degenerate into optimism. For that is the road to despair. Yet it ought never to conclude because its proper end is Heaven, the Church must dally at its work until the end is in sight. The thought of the Church is fraught with tension because the life of the Church is caught in tension. For the individual Christian and the far flung congregation alike, that is part of the reality of the Cross.'

At the end of this period in Selma he returned to College in Cambridge and then, after what was to be a final visit home, went back to Selma where he proposed to spend the summer vacation months in further Civil Rights activities. But this time the going was to become much rougher.

Jon Daniels was fast approaching his eventual martyrdom when he decided, with others, to join a demonstration in Lowndes County, an area between the state capital of Alabama, Montgomery, and Selma. In terms of Civil Rights this was a most backward area, largely Negro. All of them underpaid and unrepresented, and none had acquired the right to be on the Voting Register. Some of these people had already attempted to get themselves on this Register, but had been intimidated from doing so. One of the methods of intimidation used was for the white authorities to allow blacks seeking registration to assemble in the old Jail House where the gallows stood in the very room in which they were supposed to fill out registration papers. Some few managed to do this; all were threatened during the process. It was an area in which the Ku Klux Klan, with its hooded

101

figures and its flaming Cross was active. There was bitter hatred in evidence everywhere, levelled not only against the Negro people, but in particular against those who were working with them. The degree of courage required by such people as Jonathan Daniels and those with him cannot be understood unless this terrible atmosphere, of ever present threat, is understood. To so emotional and highly strung a person as Daniels himself this must have been a terrible time. Two colleagues who travelled with him on this last trip noticed how he drove very fast in a high-powered car he had acquired. He explained to them that he needed the speed to get away from those whom he knew were pursuing him because he had already been shot at. Yet he persisted in wearing his clerical collar, thus making himself conspicuous everywhere as he rushed about the countryside, in and out of Negro houses, onto Negro farms, talking, explaining to older blacks, more timid than their young people, what were their rights and how and why they should exercise them.

One of the purposes of the planned demonstration in Lowndes County was to encourage this older element among the population. It was supported by young, and increasingly militant, blacks. Jonathan heard about it when he was not far away in Birmingham attending a Southern Christian Leadership Conference. There he met two other clergy, a young Roman Catholic Priest, Father Richard Morrisroe from Chicago, and John Ruskin Clark, a Unitarian Minister from California. These three decided to go to Lowndes County and join the demonstration. The actual location where it was to take place was Fort Deposit, the largest town in Lowndes County.

The scene there on the morning of the demonstration was highly dramatic. It was very hot; about a hundred blacks had queued outside the Post Office waiting to register to vote. Moving slowly up and down the street were the cars of white people filled with dangerous resentment. Those in charge of the young peoples' demonstration, including the celebrated Stokely Carmichael, famed in the Civil Rights Movement, urged their group to remain non-violent. All were warned by a man from the Justice Department that an armed crowd was assembling in town to oppose them. He urged them to disperse; but they refused, all were intent on moving into Fort Deposit to demonstrate outside two shops and a cafe which had become notorious for their ill treatment of Negro people. There was no stopping the determination of the demonstrators now.

All piled into a truck which drove them into the town. Daniels and Father Morrisroe went with them. In the town, in the baking noon day, they were met by a crowd of white men armed with sticks. When the demonstrators tried to assemble in front of the three chosen locations, they were moved on, always nearer and nearer to the crowd of men. It could have been the moment of flash-point; but instead five police officers stopped the demonstrators, arresting them on a charge of disturbing the peace. The whole group was loaded into another truck and driven to the County Jail in Haynesville. On the way there the prisoners sang; when they were in the Jail they could be heard still singing. Meanwhile Civil Rights workers in Selma went to work to secure the release of the prisoners, raising bail, trying to find a lawyer to handle the case, and exerting pressures upon local official-dom. But the threatening atmosphere persisted in the district. The presence of the Ku Klux Klan was sensed; there was an impression of a burnt Cross on the lawn of the Court House itself.

John Clark, the Unitarian Minister, who had not been with the demonstrators, visited the Jail in Haynesville and found Jon Daniels in good heart, held in a cell with Stokely Carmichael and two other blacks. Father Morrisroe was in another cell nearby. All were in good spirits. They had been there almost a week when, quite suddenly and without any apparent reason, all were released, on condition of leaving the county. So, at about three o'clock in the afternoon, the whole party found themselves outside the jail in the hostile street. Until they could be picked up by friends, all were in a dangerous and vulnerable situation.

Across the street from where they were standing was a grocery store, and towards this, with the intention of buying something to eat and drink, Jon Daniels, Father Morrisroe, and two girls who had been in the demonstration walked over. They were half way up the steps of the store when a man came out pointing a gun at them and yelling: 'Goddam Niggers, get off this property before I blow your damned brains out!' He fired, and Jon Daniels, shot in the stomach, fell, pouring blood. There was another shot, and Father Morrisroe fell. Before Jon was shot he had managed to pull the girl with him to the ground, and she survived. Jon had been killed instantly by the shotgun. Father Morrisroe, shot in the back, was gravely wounded yet lay in the street for an hour before being taken to hospital. The rest of those who had been arrested and then released had fled: cars continued to move up and down the street; but none of them stopped. The man who had done the shooting walked over to the Court House to telephone Montgomery with the news of what he had done. He was a man of 55, Thomas L. Coleman, member of a well known Alabama family and a Deputy Sheriff. He was arrested, and held for trial. Father Morrisroe was operated on in the Baptist Hospital in Montgomery throughout the night. Jonathan Daniels was dead.

His death came as a great shock to many. His Bishop said: 'Jonathan gave his life for the enlightenment and rights of his fellow men. All of us who knew him, loved him . . . it is easy to be bitter about his death, but Jonathan would resist such bitterness and call us instead to a deeper compassion and understanding of those he died to serve, both White and Negroes.' Father Morrisroe's people in Chicago were equally hit hard. On the other hand, there was a Deputy Sheriff in Haynesville who, according to a New York Herald Tribune reporter, said: 'I hope the son of a bitch dies. That'll give us two of them instead of just one.' It was a bad time: not more than two days after the killing of Jonathan and the shooting of Morrisroe, another clergyman, the 59-year-old Donald Thomson of the first Unitarian Church of Jackson, was gravely wounded by gunfire from three men waiting for him in a car. Morrisroe slowly recovered and while doing so sent a message from hospital saying that he felt no hatred towards the man who had shot him.

That man, Tom Coleman, was eventually placed on trial in Haynesville on a charge of first degree manslaughter. An all white jury, after a tumultuous trial, in the course of which the false claim was made that Jon Daniels had been carrying a knife at the time of his shooting, acquitted Coleman on all charges and he walked out of the court a free man.

But the instruments of martyrdom, the men who actually bring it about, like those who hanged Bonhoeffer, or who put Maximilian Kolbe in the death cell at Auschwitz, are unimportant, and soon fade from memory. But Jon Daniels, by his dying, lives on. At a service for him back in Keene, New Hampshire, the Principal of his Theological School read some words which Jon had written. He had been trying, it seemed, to work out why some Civil Rights workers seemed self-righteous, why some who were involved in non-violence said that they loved their persecutors and at the same time felt hostility towards them. He was concerned to think how such mixed motivations could be related to that act of perfect love in which Christ on the Cross gave himself for all men. Then he wrote these words of himself:

'I lost fear in the black belt when I began to know in my bones and sinews that I had truly been baptized into the Lord's death and resurrection, and in the only sense that really mattered I am already dead, and my life is hid with Christ in God. I began to lose self-righteousness when I discovered the extent to which my behaviour was motivated by worldly desires. . . . The point is simply, of course, that one's motives are usually mixed – and one had better know it. It occurred to me that though I was reasonably certain that I was in Selma because the Holy Spirit had sent me

105

there, there remained a fundamental distinction between my will and his. "And Holy is his name," I was reminded . . . that I am called first to holiness. Every impulse, every motive, every will under Heaven must attend first to that if it is to be healthy and free. . . .'

In the Chapel of Saints and Martyrs of Our Own Time in Canterbury Cathedral there is an entry: 'Jonathan Daniels, died 1965. Student of the Episcopal Theological School in Cambridge, Massachusetts. Shot in Haynesville, Alabama, while helping in the Civil Rights Campaign; gave his life to save one of his companions.'

A more famous man was to die in the same cause three years later.

11
MAN WITH A VISION

MARTIN LUTHER KING, who became internationally famed as a dominant figure in the Civil Rights movement in the US had a vision for his people of justice and freedom. He died violently in 1968 before he saw it fulfilled. But he left an inspiring memory; as an advocate of non-violence. Like that of Gandhi, his example is of continuing importance.

The traffic was heavy on the afternoon of 1 December 1955, in Montgomery, Alabama. An elderly black woman, Rosa Parkes, found there was just room for her in the seats at the back of a bus reserved for those of her colour. Whites were always seated at the front. A few stops later a white man boarded; but there was no seat left for him. The driver ordered Mrs Parkes, sitting quietly on her wooden seat holding her shopping basket, to stand and surrender her seat. She refused. The driver summoned police who arrested Mrs Parkes on the spot and took her to the police office. What was unusual about this police action was not the action itself, but that of the woman who had caused it. Given the state of race relations in Alabama, as in other Southern states at that time, it was quite common for a black to be turned off a bus in favour of a white passenger. In fact, not long before, a black had been shot dead by police when asking for the return of fare when told that there was no seat for him.

But times had been gradually changing. Some other black women had refused to surrender their seats only a little while before the incident of Mrs Parkes. But maybe because she was a well known citizen, and certainly a respectable one, her case, in a modest way at first, caught public attention, and was featured in the paper, the Montgomery Advertiser.

There it was seen by a black minister called Martin Luther King. He, in company with other colleagues, resolving that the time had come for action, offered his church building for protest meetings. Mrs Parkes had started something bigger than she knew.

Soon, black citizens had received notices asking them not to ride any bus to work, or to town, or to school, or any place at all on the day chosen for a bus boycott, which had been organized for Monday, 5 December. The result was astonishing. Before long the 'bus company was in serious difficulties as their vehicles travelled almost empty. A year later, so extensive had become the nationwide repercussions of this incident that the almost unbelievable happened. The United States Supreme Court ruled that segregation by race in 'buses was illegal under the American Constitution. Martin Luther King, increasingly seen as the key figure in what was to become a massive Campaign for the Advancement of Coloured People, with international off-shoots of all kinds, had had his home bombed, his family threatened and he himself had been to jail for a conscience-inspired non-payment of a fine. This was the man who before long was to receive a Nobel Prize, to have a vision of the future of his people, and to die a martyr's death by gunshot on the balcony of a motel in Memphis, Tennessee.

Mrs Rosa Parkes, who had been arrested on the 'bus, had been, as a commentator put it, 'anchored to her seat by the accumulated indignities of days gone by and by the boundless aspiration of generations yet unborn'. The negro population of America's South had indeed suffered indignities for many generations. Their background lay in the slave society of the Southern States, whose tobacco and cotton crops had by long tradition been worked by such labour, brought in originally chiefly from Africa by the slave trade. It was an established thing, a way of life. Slavery had been one of the great issues of the American Civil War when the city of Montgomery, the very place where Mrs Parkes was arrested that day in 1955, had been the first State capital of the Confederacy to react fiercely to the proposal of the Federal Government of the US ultimately to abolish slavery. And though the Southern States of the Confederacy were in that War defeated, their laws overall had not become more liberal: the segregation of black and white had been rigorously maintained, and the economic and social disadvantages of the black people had been in almost all respects continued.

Such was the background to the struggle in which Martin Luther King gave his life. He was not himself in any way a 'poor black'. His home in Atlanta, Georgia, was highly respectable; his father Minister of the well known Ebenezer Baptist Church. Here, after his marriage to Coretta, the woman who was to share his subsequent fame and many of his sufferings, he became after ordination assistant to his father. It says a great deal about the state of racial prejudice in the Southern States, however, that once, when Martin with a friend entered a restaurant for a meal with two girls, they were all turned out, the proprietor firing a revolver into the air to stress his point.

The famous 'bus boycott in Montgomery, Alabama marked the beginning for Martin of what was to be a long and involved struggle which was to have lasting effects not only upon the society and laws of the United States itself, but upon world thinking in many lands upon the whole matter of race. The young minister from Atlanta was, in the course of time, to meet the Pope, to preach in St Pauls, to visit India, to receive the Nobel Peace Prize, to become an international figure. But it was the creed of non-violent resistance at the heart of his conduct and beliefs, which made the greatest and most lasting mark. It was a creed difficult to maintain as time went by, when the younger generation of blacks came to feel that violence would achieve greater and quicker results than non-violence. But on this question King never wavered, costly as was his determination. Non-violence, he once said, was 'a courageous confrontation

109

of evil by the power of love, in the faith that it is better to be the recipient of violence than the inflictor of it.' The inspiration came directly from the teachings and example of Jesus. 'You have learned that they were told, "An eye for an eye, and a tooth for a tooth." What I tell you is this: do not set yourself against the man who wrongs you. If someone slaps you on the right cheek, turn and offer him your left. . . . You have learned that they were told, "Love your neighbour, hate your enemy." But what I tell you is this: Love your enemies and pray for your persecutors; only so can you be children of your Heavenly Father.' (Matt. 5.39: 40: 43–45.)

He was also deeply impressed by the example of Gandhi, in his non-resistance campaign against British rule in India. When Martin visited that country, where he met with Prime Minister Nehru, he said; 'To other countries I may go as a tourist, but to India I come as a pilgrim. This is because India means to me Mahatma Gandhi, a truly great man of the age.' He had already, in a speech back home in the US before this India visit, made very plain his own message of non-violence: 'It is my hope that as the Negro plunges deeper into the quest for freedom and justice he will plunge even deeper into the philosophy of non–violence. The Negro all over the South must come to the point that he can say to his white brother: "We will match your capacity to inflict suffering with our capacity to endure suffering. We will meet your physical force with soul force. We will not hate you, but we will not obey your evil Laws. We will soon wear you down by pure capacity to suffer."'

He had already by that time himself endured suffering. There had been further imprisonments. There was a nearly fatal stabbing attack on him when he visited Harlem, in New York City. As he was autographing copies of his first book *Stride Towards Freedom*, a woman plunged an eight inch dagger into his chest, an assault from which, surprisingly, he recovered, remaining calm throughout the whole ordeal as he sat in the department store where it had happened with

110

the dagger still in his chest. He told his doctors that he had had 'divine companionship' in the struggle, and that this was the source of his strength.

The course of that struggle was long and involved. It was also costly in terms of spiritual effort to Martin himself, a highly emotional man. Perhaps it was this emotional tendency which caused him to alarm his followers by a strange outburst at the height of the Montgomery 'bus boycott struggle when he suddenly shouted in the middle of a prayer: 'Lord, I hope no one will die as a result of our struggle for freedom in Montgomery. Certainly I don't want to die. But if anyone has to die, let it be me.' No one at the time saw the significance of the words.

He was a gifted orator, a great preacher very much in the tradition of the preachers of the black South who were required to stir their congregations by strong words richly expressed. But Martin brought to his oratory something else – a prophetic vision for his people and for their freedom which had staggering effects upon those who heard him, and which still remains in the collective memory, with the power to stir, long after the particular circumstances which gave rise to the words have passed away. This was particularly true of what became known as his 'I have a dream' speech. The place was Washington, the date Wednesday, 28 August 1963. A crowd estimated at something like a quarter of a million had gathered around the Lincoln Monument. It was the culmination of a vast non-violent demonstration in the cause of Civil Rights for Coloured People; but it was attended by many thousands of whites also. Martin, who had spent much anxious preparation over what he knew would be a key speech, altered it almost at the last minute in order that it should draw some of its inspiration from the very memorial to Abraham Lincoln towering before them. On the plinth of that statue are carved the words of the Declaration of Independence: 'We hold these truths to be self-evident, that all men are created equal. . . .' Martin continued, standing there in the humid

Washington heat with the crowd suddenly hushed before him: 'Five score years ago a great American, in whose symbolic shadow we stand, signed the Emancipation Proclamation. But one hundred years later we must face the tragic fact that the Negro is still not free. One hundred years later, the life of the Negro is still sadly crippled by the manacles of segregation and the chains of discrimination. One hundred years later the Negro lives on a lonely island of poverty in the midst of a vast ocean of material prosperity. . . . There will be neither rest nor tranquillity in America until the Negro is granted his citizenship rights. The whirlwinds of revolt will continue to shake the foundations of our nation until the bright day of justice emerges.' And then he told them that he had a dream. It was that, one day, the nation would really practise its creed, that 'All men are created equal.' He said he dreamt that the children of slaves and of slave owners would one day live in brotherhood. He had a dream, he went on, that one day his four little children would be judged not by their colour but by their character. He had a dream – and here he went straight into the language of the Old Testament in the words of the prophet Isaiah: 'I have a dream that one day every valley shall be exalted, every hill and mountain shall be made low, the rough places will be made plain and the crooked places will be made straight, and the Glory of the Lord shall be revealed, and all flesh shall see it together. This will be the day when all God's children will be able to sing with new meaning "My country 'tis of thee, sweet land of liberty, of thee I sing. Land where my fathers died, land of the pilgrim's pride." When we let freedom ring' he concluded, 'when we let it ring from every village and every hamlet, from every state and every city, we will be able to speed up that day when all God's children, black men and white men, Jews and Gentiles, Protestants and Catholics, will be able to join hands and sing in the words of that old Negro spiritual: "Free at Last! Free at last! Thank God Almighty, we are free at last!"'

This was an historic speech; but it still left the American

scene burdened with its weight of race prejudice and apathy, especially in the South. A distinguished American, Senator Hubert Humphrey, who watched and listened that day with over 150 other members of Congress, said afterwards that: 'All this probably hasn't changed any votes on the Civil Rights Bill, but its a good thing for Washington and the Nation and the World.'

The following year Martin Luther King received the Nobel Peace Prize in Norway. On his way there he preached in St Paul's Cathedral, the first non-Anglican ever to occupy its pulpit. Altogether he had three days of speeches before going on to Oslo, attracting capacity audiences everywhere and addressing Members of Parliament. But it was in his St Pauls sermon, and later in his Nobel Prize address, that he again pronounced the principles upon which he acted. In St Paul's, his theme was from Revelations 21, with its vision of the Holy City: his particular text was 'Its length and breadth and height being equal.' (Rev. 21:16.)

'Love yourself, if that means healthy self interest . . . That is the length of life. Love your neighbour as yourself; you are commanded to do that . . . That is the breadth of life. But never forget that there is an even greater Commandment, "Love the Lord your God with all your heart, and with all your soul, and with all your mind." That is the height of life. God grant that we may move with unrelenting passion towards that city of complete life in which the length and breadth and the height are equal.'

On Thursday, 10 December 1964, in the Auditorium of Oslo University, Martin was much moved as the Chairman of the Nobel Committee referred to him as: 'an undaunted champion of peace . . . First person in the Western World to have shown us that a struggle can be waged without violence.' When it came to his time to reply he began by saying 'I accept the Nobel Prize for Peace for at a moment when 22 million Negroes of the United States of America are engaged in a creative battle to end the long night of racial injustice . . . I am mindful that debilitating and grinding poverty afflicts my people and chains them to the lowest rung of the economic ladder.' Then he widened his words to include the whole question of the threat of violence which overhung the whole world, especially in a time of nuclear weaponry. One of the first to pronounce in this way upon this issue, he said that it was essential to believe that man was not a helpless drifter in the river of existence but an active agent in the unfolding events by which he was surrounded. He denied passionately the notion that the nations of the world must necessarily 'spiral down a materialistic staircase into the hall of thermo-nuclear destruction.' And then he stated again the very core of his philosophy: 'I believe that unarmed truth and unconditional love will have the final word in reality.'

But these honours and these plaudits of the wider world could not conceal the fact that, back home in the Southern States opposition and, as events were to prove, mortal dangers, still confronted King. When he returned from Oslo after receiving this Nobel Prize, he was given a triumphant reception in New York where the Mayor of the City honoured him and the Vice-President of the United States attended a banquet in his honour. Yet this was only a plane flight away from a scene of an entirely different nature to which Martin next passed in Selma, Alabama. This was a Black Belt City 'over which,' as an American writer has said, 'the stench of slavery hung densely, as yet undisturbed by the winds of change that were sweeping through other parts of the South.'

The Sheriff of Selma was a notorious figure, Jim Clark, a huge man known for his tough repression of all black agitation. The cause which brought King to Jim Clark's town was the fact that Selma's blacks had long been excluded from the Electoral Registration Rolls, so that they were disenfranchised, apart from a bare one per cent, in a place where there were more than 15,000 of them. It was Martin's purpose to speak on behalf of black voting rights. It was a tense situation, watched by many Western journalists and by the whole of the United States itself. Martin registered at an hotel hitherto always reserved for whites only. In the lobby he was attacked by a white who was wrestled to the ground and taken away. Then he led a crowd marching toward the Selma Courthouse to register. Here he came face to face with Jim Clark himself. They were turned away on the excuse that there were no Registrars on duty; but everyone knew that this was but the beginning of what was to be a bitter campaign. When, later, Martin led a demonstration towards the Selma Courthouse, he was arrested along with 770 of the demonstrators. On the following day 550 more were arrested, and there were those who prophesied a massacre of blacks by whites.

It nearly came to that. There was an occasion later in the Selma campaign when a procession of more than 500 of Martin's followers, accompanied by many white Christians, marched from their Chapel intending to demonstrate in Montgomery. They were attacked by Sheriff Clark's forces with gas, cattle prods and clubs as they charged on horseback into the crowd. Many were injured, some very seriously. Eventually the marchers were persuaded to re-enter the church from which they had come and to take refuge; but many, ominously, were speaking of the need to retaliate. Never was the need greater for Martin to maintain his principle of non-violence, and to persuade his followers that this continued to be the right way. He had not been present at this particular disturbance, because he was away in Atlanta. But he was very much involved in the tremendous climax to the whole Selma happening when he led the march at the head of a crowd of thousands from that town into the State capital of Montgomery. Attempts by the opposition, reaching up to the President of the United States himself, had been made to prevent this march. But Governor Wallace of Alabama was not successful, and President Johnson authorized what was to follow.

So it came about that King led the march, with the words: 'Walk together, children; don't you get weary, and it will lead us to the Promised Land. And Alabama will be a new Alabama, and America will be a new America.' Singing 'We shall overcome,' the famous anthem of the Civil Rights Movement, the whole mass started along US Highway 80. Nothing like it had evern been seen before, and not many events in the history of the US had more far-reaching results. The exhilaration of the Selma-Montgomery March, accompanied as it was by many distinguished citizens, including an Episcopal Bishop of California, a Rabbi of the American–Jewish Theological Seminary, the President of the New York City Council and many others was immense. So was the impression made by the host of actors, singers, and show business people who came to lend their support. And eventually they got there, and the battle was won.

Martin hailed the occasion with memorable words again: 'They told us we wouldn't get here. But all the world together knows that we are here and that we are standing before the forces of power in the State of Alabama. . . . My people, my people, listen! The battle is in our hands. I know some of you are asking today, "How long will it take!" I say to you that, however difficult the moment, however frustrating the hour, it will not be long, because truth pressed to earth will rise again. How long? Not long, because no lie can live forever. How long? Not long, because you will reap what you sow. How long? Not long, because the arm of the moral universe is long but bends towards justice. How long? Not long, because mine eyes have seen the glory of the coming of the Lord, trampling out the vintage where the grapes of wrath are stored. He has loosed the fateful lightening of his terrible swift sword. His truth is marching on.'

But it had been a costly victory, and not only for Martin. Some of his white supporters suffered too. A Mrs Viola Liuzzo, a housewife and mother of five, who had been a march supporter, was shot dead as she was driving her car back from Montgomery to Selma with a young black man as passenger. The incident, which aroused National indig-

116

nation, was some indication of the continuing bitter opposition which the Civil Rights Movement had aroused, which it was to go on arousing, and which had claimed some lives already. Eventually, it was to cost King his own.

The end came in the town of Memphis, Tennessee where he had gone on a preaching and speaking engagement. He was at the height of his fame; but, strangely, he seemed to have a premonition of his end. He said to his congregation, in words which puzzled and silenced them, 'I don't know what will happen now. But it doesn't really matter with me now. Because I have been to the mountain top. I won't mind. Like anybody, I would like to live a long life; longevity has its place. But I am not concerned about that now. I just want to do God's will. And he has allowed me to go up to the mountain. And I have looked over, and I have seen the Promised Land. I may not get there with you; but I want you to know tonight that we as a people will get to that Promised Land. So I am happy tonight. I am not worried about anything. I am not fearing any man. "Mine eyes have seen the glory of the coming of the Lord".'

Martin's party was staying in a place called the Lorraine Motel. That evening he was to have gone out to dinner with a ministerial colleague. But he did not know that, into a seedy transient hotel opposite the Lorraine, a man calling himself John Willard had booked himself. He was armed with a Remington telescopic rifle, a box of soft nosed bullets, and a pair of binoculars. He had access to a balcony looking straight across the street to that of Martin's room. Shortly after 6 p.m., Martin appeared on his balcony and Willard shot him through the face. Eight minutes later Martin Luther King was dead.

Beyond a doubt, he was a great man, not so much in character – because he had his weaknesses – not so much in achievement because, vast though it was, the cause of justice for the blacks of America might have been achieved, in so far as it has been wholly achieved, by the general progress of events. His greatness lay rather in the steadfastness with which he held to his profoundly Christian principles of action, based on the teachings of Christ and upon, above all, the principle of non-violence. Through those principles he was able to arouse the conscience of the world. For those principles and for that devotion, he died a martyr's death.

In Uganda, in the following year, another great man was to do likewise.

12
THE EMPTY GRAVE

The memory of the fearful time of tyranny under the Presidency of Idi Amin in Uganda is still vivid. It claimed many lives. One of them was that of the courageous leader JANANI LUWUM, Archbishop of Uganda, whose death added yet another name to the long roll of Ugandan martyrs.

There is a tradition, and a vivid memory of martyrdom in Uganda, which runs like a red streak across the country's Christian history. Some understanding of that tradition is important to the story of Janani Luwum, Archbishop of Uganda, who was himself martyred on 17 February 1977 at the hands of Idi Amin, at that time Uganda's tyrant ruler.

That same year, 1977, was the centenary of the first coming of Christianity to Uganda, and its first martyrs had gone to their deaths within ten years of the coming, first of the Church Missionary Society's missionaries under Alexander Mackay, and then of a Roman Catholic party of White Fathers under Fr Lourdel. The fact that the rivalry between these two groups was intense has not impaired the splendour of it. When the first martyrs came to suffer, they did so together, young pages at the Court of the King of Buganda, the Kabaka. These were the celebrated 'Boy Martyrs' who, bound together and wrapped in rush mats, were burned alive after a forced march to the Royal execution site at Namagongo. The date was 3 June 1886. Before the fires were lit each boy was asked to name the charge against him for which he was to die. Without exception, each answered 'for following Christ'.

The intelligent young men who had been chosen as pages were from the first keen listeners to what the missionaries had to tell them, and the Gospel came to them as something in dramatic contrast to the barbarities which they saw all around them at Court. The cruelties of the Kabaka had shocked first Victorian explorers, such as Speke who, in their searches for the source of the Nile, had been the first Europeans to enter this remote kingdom almost in the middle of Africa. Life was cheap; the authority of the King absolute, and a nod from him in the direction of any particular courtier was sufficient to send the royal executioner to drag the designated victim outside to be decapitated. In the eyes of these early European visitors, as of the missionaries afterwards, it made the picture all the more tragic that the Bugandans were a charming Nilotic people with a cultural standard far higher than that of the African peoples around them.

In the strange way in which the pattern of martyrdom in Uganda seems to have repeated itself, there was a tyrant ruler responsible for driving these victims to their deaths, just as there was in the case of Janani Luwum a century later. The earlier tyrant was the Kabaka Mwanga, who had succeeded his more accommodating father, Mutesa, who, for all his cruelties, had permitted the baptism of some of his pages. But with Mwanga all that was brought to an end. Pages were seized at random and sent to their deaths. One of them, the first Catholic martyr, Joseph Balikuddempe, was even one of the Kabaka's favourites. The mass killing of the boys took place when the King, returning unexpectedly from a hunt, discovered most of his pages studying the Scriptures. A great fear descended upon the Court. Those implicated encouraged each other with words of the Gospel which had come to them through the translation of Alexander Mackay: 'Everyone who acknowledges me before me, I also will acknowledge before my Father who is in Heaven' (Matt. 10:32) and: 'Blessed are those who are persecuted for righteousness sake, for theirs is the Kingdom of Heaven.' (Matt. 5:4.) These pages were they, who, Anglicans and Catholics alike, suffered together when the time came.

One of those who suffered had bravely accused the

Kabaka of unjustly plotting the death of James Hannington, the Anglican Bishop who was martyred in 1885, when he was murdered by natives as he leading an expedition to open up a shorter route to Lake Victoria Nyanza. Such, then, was the considerable tradition of martyrdom which was strong in the Church in Uganda when Janani Luwum, a hundred years later, became its Archbishop.

Physically, he was a huge man, typical of the Acholi Tribe whose territory, far to the North was on the Border of the Sudan. Chiefly a cattle keeping people, they lived a ranging life, herding their beasts, the women tending the crops around the family homesteads. Janani grew up in these surroundings and was, in his physical powers, very much a product of them. But he also inherited something else: a Christian background. His father had been an early convert and was a Church teacher, a layman who had given his life to Christ. They were very poor; but the father was undauntedly faithful. From this home Janani, as a young man, went to the Boroboro Teacher Training College based on a nearby Mission Station. Here he did well, receiving high commendations and eventually passed out as a qualified teacher in 1942 and was sent to a primary school in the eastern part of his country.

Janani became a Christian at a specific time and place, 6 January 1948. There had been a mission in his home village, presented by revivalist movement whose followers were called Balokole. In their simplicity, and in the rigour of the challenge which they presented to their listeners – to change their lives, to cast out their sins, to devote themselves utterly to Christ – there was an air of the early Church. To these people the Holy Spirit was one who convicted, who took hold of peoples' lives, however outwardly these might have been conforming to a Christian pattern, and called upon them in spirit and in truth to look into those lives and perceive how they had fallen short of the challenge to repent and believe the Gospel and be saved. There was nothing half-hearted or restrained about this kind of preaching or

121

about its results. When these came, they could be dynamic and startling. When the sense of his own sins and of the promise of Christ to free him from them came upon Janani himself, he sweated, confessed Christ as his Lord, wept, crying so loudly that people in the village ran to see. They were to hear his testimony: 'Today I have become a leader in Christ's Army. I am prepared to die in the Army of Jesus. As Jesus shed his blood for the people, if it is God's will, I will do the same.' He could scarcely have known how utterly that was to come to pass.

For a year after this conversion experience he identified himself strongly with this revivalist movement. It was all the harder a road to follow because the movement itself was by no means wholly acceptable to the Church. There were leaders who saw it as unnecessarily divisive. For Janani himself, as a teacher in a Church school, it presented especial difficulties. It could bring him, very understandably, into trouble with authority because he could be accused and in fact was so accused, of going beyond his duties to challenge his pupils with the message of repentance. This led to his dismissal from one school. Later, with others, he was arrested on a charge of disturbing the peace. Here again was a scene strongly reminiscent of New Testament accounts of imprisonment, even to the point of the taunting of the warders. When these asked their prisoners to denounce their faith it was Janani who replied: 'You are good people and our beloved brothers. It is not you, but your master, Satan, who is using you to torture us and leave us to go hungry. We love you, and our master, Jesus Christ, loves you too. The wooden bars at the window of this cell cannot separate us from the love of God, nor stop us proclaiming his message of salvation, through his son Jesus Christ. All of us here are committed to Christ, even unto death.' And then they all together thanked God that they had been found worthy to suffer for the sake of Christ.

All this belonged to the early stages of Luwum's Christian experience. He was to discover, as the years went by, and new horizons opened before him, that such utter simplicities were not always the Lord's way, and that the governance of the Church, and the sustaining of the will of its people, usually called for a less uncompromising but always for a loving approach. However, for the moment, he stayed with the Balokole, and the Movement grew to a point where there seemed a real danger of it causing a schism within the Church. Church leaders were deeply disturbed. Would it not be better, they considered, for some of the Balokole themselves to seek further education in order that they could speak with greater authority within the Church itself, rather than, as sometimes appeared to be happening, encouraging the conditions in which people might be tempted to break away? Those among them who felt that this was the way ahead looked to the young teacher, Janani Luwum. Would he, they asked, abandon his teaching career and train to become a Pastor of the Anglican Church? He consented, and so joined the first course for Lay Readers conducted in English at Buwalasi Theological College. He had set out on the path which was not only to provide him with much further education, to send him overseas to England but which was, ultimately, to lead to his martyrdom.

At the end of his course, in 1950, Janani and his wife, who had joined him in the Theological College, returned to his Acholi homeland. There he worked as a Lay Reader in St Philips Church, Gulu, where his personality began to make a marked impression. He was vigorous, enthusiastic, very able, and his new found knowledge of English enabled him to act as translator at Church meetings. He was also emerging as a leader of considerable powers. In 1953 he returned to Buwalasi Theological College and in the December of 1955 was ordained deacon and the following year, priest.

The need of the Church in Uganda was for more Ugandans to lead it. How were such men to be given the further training which would be necessary? The answer came through the initiative of an English clergyman, the

Revd Neville Sugden, Vicar of St Marys, Shortlands, in Kent, who, when the Bishop who had ordained Janani was visiting, asked him if he knew anyone who might benefit from a year's course in England. The Bishop, Keith Russell, replied that he did indeed know such a man. So it came about that, in the January of 1958, Janani came to England.

He went for a one year course at St Augustine's College, Canterbury, then the central College of the Anglican Communion. Here totally new vistas of experience and understanding opened before him as this massive Acholi man, with his origins in a remote part of Northern Uganda, found his mind exposed to a wider range of Christian thinking than ever it had hitherto encountered. In 1959 he returned to Uganda where he was appointed to work in a parish in East Acholi, a parish forty miles in extent, with twenty-four daughter churches and its Priest equipped only with a bicycle. There he had a difficult time, not because of these physical challenges; but because the soil upon which he sought to sow the seed of faith had become infertile. People were for the time being more interested in politics than the Christian faith or any other. Yet his life in this first parish had its rewards, even if they did not appear until years later. There was one occasion when some young men of the parish burnt down a church. Janani forgave them. Years later, one of them said that his attitude of forgiveness had helped that very young man, now one of the leaders of the Church in Uganda, to surrender his life to Christ.

Many important events now took place in the life of Luwum, all within a comparatively short space of time, as though the pace was quickening towards the end of his earthly story. In 1962 he became Vice-Principal of the Theological College which he had, not long before, attended as a pupil. He was there when Uganda received its independence. At the same time he returned to England, this time to study at the London College of Divinity of which, after two years very hard work, he received the Diploma. Back in Uganda, he became Principal of his College, where he was greatly loved. But he was not there long because in 1966 he became Provincial Secretary, a high appointment in the Church in Uganda. In that position, in the midst of an increasingly tumultuous political scene, his wisdom and his faith were tested severely. Even so, the Church strove greatly to expand, looking towards the year of its centenary in 1977. And in all this Luwum, now at the centre of things, was an inspiring force. In 1968 he returned for the third and last time to England as one of the Consultants to the Archbishop of Canterbury at the Lambeth Conference of that year. On his return he was appointed Bishop of Northern Uganda.

There now began an intensely active period of his life. He was loved, he was applauded; wherever he went, driving fast, the people delighted in his coming. He was known, too, for his devotion to the cause of the Lepers, a disease very active in the country. It was known that, when patients were discharged cured, as frequently happened, he would always wish to take a short Service of Thanksgiving for them in their own native tongue. This work and this concern of his, among many others, drew wide attention. 'People these days say there is no God,' a Government worker was once heard to say, 'but how ridiculous when we can see things like fellowship between races and tribes, and people getting cured of their leprosy, none of which would happen if there was not a God.' But Janani was always conscious of the spiritual dangers of such vast popularity to quote some words of Archbishop William Temple: 'My original sin is that I put myself in the centre of the picture. I don't belong there. God does.' And so, with such humility always in his heart, he struggled on, encountering sorrows as well as joys, mistakes as well as triumphs. He was not infallible; but he was unshakably faithful to his Lord and Master. Then, on the 9 June 1974 he was consecrated in Namirembe Cathedral, Archbishop of Uganda.

Meanwhile, very dark clouds indeed had been gathering over that country. A terrible series of political killings began with the attempted assassination of Milton Obote, the first President. At the same time a leading soldier, Brigadier Okoya, together with his wife, was shot. A certain General Amin was suspected of this murder, and was known to be already responsible for many others. This man, once a Sergeant in the King's African Rifles, had begun to loom over the Ugandan scene. His bodyguard had already achieved a dread reputation, and were to add to it in the years ahead. The coup which brought Amin to power came in the January of 1971 when, in the absence of President Obote at the Commonwealth Conference in Singapore, he seized power. This was the man who, probably by his own hand, was to bring about the martyrdom of Janani Luwum.

But many things were to happen in the rapid descent of Uganda into chaos before that final moment came. The maximum terror came after the coup, when Amin's troops ranged everywhere looking for former followers of Obote. The pattern of brutality which was to become so familiar soon showed itself in such actions as the public shooting of Army deserters. The Chief Justice was dismembered alive outside his own High Court. The Vice-Chancellor of Makerere University in Kampala met his death in the infamous Makindye Military Prison, where many were to perish. In such circumstances the task of a Bishop was severe indeed. Luwum, on his travels through his diocese, met often with grieving people mourning the loss of husbands, sons or brothers. The situation was made no easier by the fact that the Church itself was in an unstable condition, with feuds along tribal lines following a sadly familiar African pattern.

But if this was a difficult time to be a bishop, it was even more a challenging time to become an Archbishop. And yet, following the retirement of Archbishop Sabiti, Janani Luwum was elected to succeed him. It was an extraordinarily difficult time. The economy was in chaos; the Asians had been expelled, the British Community had long ago quietly withdrawn, and beneath the surface everywhere was terror. What is more, Muslim pressure on the Christian Church became severe. Amin himself was from a Muslim tribe – the Kakwa. Positions in the Public Administration which had formerly been held by Christians, passed into the hands of Muslims. Soon Luwum himself was accused by the President of giving aid and comfort to fleeing Government Officials. It took courage – and he had it in abundance – to give such vigorous leadership as he did in so frightful a situation, and his task was made harder by the number of people who came to him for advice and comfort.

The crisis came in the February of 1977. His house was raided in the middle of the night. As he heard his dog barking Luwum went downstairs and, on looking through his front door, saw a wounded man whom he recognized. When he opened the door three men rushed in demanding that he showed them 'the arms'. Pressed for an explanation, the wounded captive with them said that cases of arms which had been brought into the country had been found in his own house, that he had been involved in this action and that he would die for it. But only half the weapons had been discovered and the soldiers thought that more would be found in Luwum's home. He said: 'There are no arms here. Our house is God's house . . . we preach the Gospel. That is our work, not keeping arms to overthrow the Government.' The soldiers found nothing and went away, taking their prisoner with them.

The news passed quickly around that their own Archbishop had been subjected to this insult and this danger. The Roman Catholic Cardinal Archbishop came to visit Janani and to condole with him. The Anglican Bishops were summoned to meet together, when they drafted a memorandum of protest. When they met a second time Luwum, reading with them a Bible passage, commended to them the story of the disciples in the storm on Galilee. As Jesus had come to his disciples then, so now, Janani told them, he would do to them. He said: 'The Lord has seen us in the past four days making headway painfully. But I see the way

127

ahead very clearly. There are storms, waves, wind and danger, but I see the road clearly.'

A few days later Amin sent for the Archbishop and, alone with him, accused him of plotting to overthrow the Government, an accusation broadcast on Radio that very day and printed in the press. This was followed by a staged trial at the International Conference Centre in Kampala. Amin, presiding, confronted the crowds he had assembled with what he held to be the evidence of captured arms. As the bishops, with other leaders, stood in the sun before him, a statement was read out which included the name of Janani Luwum, Archbishop of Uganda, as one of those who had plotted. After this confrontation, at which many had expected a mass execution on the spot, the crowd was allowed to disperse; but Luwum was commanded to go into the presence of Amin. His last words, to two of his bishops, as he turned to obey were 'I can see the hand of the Lord in this.'

No one knows exactly what happened at that interview with Amin. Some said that attempts were made to force Janani to sign a confession. Others claimed that he was heard to pray aloud for his captors. The following morning the press carried the story that the Archbishop, together with two Cabinet Ministers who were fleeing with him, had been killed in a car crash. This was certainly entirely untrue. Those who saw his body later in the mortuary noted that he had been shot, through the chest and through the mouth.

This body was never recovered by those who wished to give it burial; but a strange incident followed Morning Service the following Sunday in Namirembe Cathedral. Outside, a grave had been prepared to receive the body of Janani. But there was no body. People stood around and then, spontaneously, there arose the sound of many voices singing a hymn which had been used by the first martyrs of Uganda:

Daily, daily sing the praises

Of the city God hath made;
in the beauteous field of Eden,
Its foundation stones are laid.

Margaret Ford, who had been Janani Luwum's secretary, in her splendid account of his martyrdom, thus concludes her account of this incident; 'Then our eyes fell on the empty grave, a gaping hole in the earth. The words of the angel to the two women seeking Jesus' body flashed into our minds. "Why do you seek the living among the dead?". . . . We came away from the Service praising, healed by the revelation of the empty grave. We greeted each other, using the words of the old Easter greeting: "Christ is risen − he is risen indeed!" Archbishop Sabiti spoke to me briefly as I was leaving: "Why are we bothering about the body? Janani went straight to Heaven."'

From such a martyrdom to the death of a very different kind of African, Steve Biko in Port Elizabeth in the same year is a long step. The link is that both died under tyranny − and both for a cause.

13
CHAMPION OF HIS PEOPLE

Like Raoul Wallenburg, STEVE BIKO, whose name is one of the most recent additions to the Book of Martyrs in St Paul's Cathedral was not avowedly a practising Christian in his life. This place among the company of martyrs is warranted by his death for the cause of his fellow black South Africans in their struggle for justice.

Towards the end of 1982 a report appeared in the press to the effect that 'The Synod of Bishops of the Church of the Province of Southern Africa is about to discuss a proposal from Natal Diocesan Synod that the late Mr Steve Biko should be included in the Church's Calendar as a martyr.' It went on to report that Biko died in detention while being held by the South African Security Police in 1977. With him was a black youth worker, who died in similar circumstances. The Synod went on to resolve that, because of the witness made to the social implications of the word of God and also 'in view of the fact that they died in the hands of a repressive system' it would request the Episcopal Synod 'to examine their lives with a view to having them appear as martyrs in the Calendar of the Church of the Province of Southern Africa'.

At the same time, almost at the other end of the world, the City Council of Cardiff, in Wales, decided to name streets in a new private housing estate after black Nationalist Leaders. One of the streets was to be called 'Biko Close'. The actual event which produced these reactions was the arrest of Steve Biko on 6 September 1977 at a Security Police road block near Grahamstown in Eastern Cape Province. Taken to

Room 619 of their building in Port Elizabeth, he was handcuffed, shackled, subject to prolonged brutal interrogation, suffered brain damage, and in that condition was transported, unconscious, 750 miles to Pretoria in the back of a landrover. Of this treatment he died, and many people across the world lamented greatly. Like Raoul Wallenburg, the Swedish Diplomat, who gave his life to save those of many Hungarian Jews in 1944, Steve Biko gave his for the sake of the cause of his own people, black South Africans. Both were predominantly secular figures: but both died for a cause, that of fellow human beings in dire need of help. And since both considered their own lives of secondary importance both warrant a place among the martyrs of our time. The black priest who, in the Natal Diocesan Synod, described Biko as a Hero of the faith was therefore right, in so far as that Christian faith involves always the duty of love and service of others.

But his faith cannot be judged, nor the claim made for him to be included in the blessed company of the martyrs, cannot be evaluated without some understanding of the circumstances which led up to his death, and of the struggle in which he, together with many other black South Africans, was involved.

South Africa, a powerful country, has throughout its history known racial tensions not only between blacks and whites, but also between whites and whites. The Afrikaners – the White Tribe, as a recent television programme described them – evolved from a merging together of the original Dutch settlers who arrived in the seventeenth century, with later comers from Germany and France, the latter as fugitives from religious persecution. These people evolved their own language – Afrikaans – their own culture, and in particular the characteristic suspicion of outside influences. Inevitably, these Afrikaners came into conflict with the British settlers who came following the annexation by Britain of the Colony following the Napoleonic Wars. In particular, the somewhat more liberal attitude of these to the black South African caused tensions over many years. It was as a reaction against these liberal tendencies, which had included the abolition of slavery, that the Afrikaners made their Great Trek which led to the foundation of the two independent Republics in the North of the country, the Transvaal, and the Orange Free State.

The events at the beginning of this century, the discovery of gold in the Transvaal, the demands of those whom this development brought to Afrikaans controlled areas in the North, culminating in the Boer War, belong to history. So does the attempted settlement of that conflict with the attempt to create in South Africa a united White nation – The Union of South Africa. So again does the rise of the Nationalist Party with its characteristic programme of Apartheid – a racial policy which has aroused a conscience, and particularly the Christian conscience of the world. But what has to a lesser degree, so far, engaged world attention is the rise of Black consciousness in South Africa.

This is a fact, which will loom inevitably larger as the years go by. Numerically, the black population of South Africa has always greatly exceeded that of the white. Yet the rise of political consciousness among this black population has been a relatively recent development. The whole shape of South African society; the force and conviction with which the policy of Apartheid is maintained, the years of suppression which have conditioned black people to regard it as natural and inevitable are all elements which have made the development of this consciousness extremely difficult. But it is a process which for many years, was marked by attempts, largely pacific, by politically conscious blacks to achieve a just share, with the whites, in the life and government of South Africa. It has been not so much a search for black domination as a resistance to white domination. The story of black politics in South Africa throughout this century is too extensive a matter to be featured here. But, in human terms, the struggle has had its heroes and its martyrs.

One of the greatest of them all was Nelson Mandela, at

one time a lawyer in Johannesburg. Following a police raid on the Headquarters of the African Nationalist Congress he was sentenced to life imprisonment on Robben Island, where he has been now for almost twenty years. His successor, in the opinion of many was, until his death, Steve Biko.

He was born in Kingwilliamstown in 1946. While still a very young man he formed the South African Students Organization, and organized and wrote for the cause until he was banned in the March of 1973. All the time he was particularly concerned with the building up of pride and awareness among his own people, by showing the worth of African culture, and by intelligent study of the ways by which the black people had been robbed of their freedom by the white settler. His call to religious leaders to support the cause of black consciousness by restoring direction and meaning to the black man's understanding of God made a great impact. Before long, his was a name to be reckoned with, not only among politically conscious black people, but within South Africa in general.

In a remarkable address at his funeral, Bishop Desmond Tutu said: 'God called Steve Biko to be his servant in South Africa – to speak up on behalf of God, declaring what the will of this God must be in a situation such as ours, a situation of evil, injustice, oppression and exploitation. God called him to be the founder father of the Black Consciousness Movement against which we have had tirades and fulminations. It is a Movement by which God, through Steve, sought to awaken in the black person a sense of his intrinsic value and worth as a child of God, not needing to apologize for his condition as a black person, calling on blacks to glorify and praise God that he had created them black.'

Steve Biko, with his brilliant mind that always saw to the heart of things, realized that until blacks asserted their humanity and their personhood, there was not the remotest chance for reconciliation in South Africa. For true reconcili-

134

ation is a deeply personal matter. It can happen only between persons who assert their own personhood, and who acknowledge and respect that of others. Steve knew and believed fervently that being pro-black was not the same thing as being anti-white. The Black Consciousness Movement is not a Hate White Movement. He had a far too profound respect for persons as persons, to want to deal with them under ready made, shop soiled categories.

All who met him had this tremendous sense of a warmhearted man, and as a notable acquaintance of his told me, 'a man who was utterly indestructable, of massive intellect and yet reticent; quite unshakeable in his commitment to principle and to radical change in South Africa by peaceful means; a man of real reconciliation, truly an instrument of God's peace, unshakeable in his commitment to the liberation of all South Africans, black and white, striving for a more just and more open South Africa.'

A picture of him from another angle comes from a journalist, Donald Woods, who became an intimate friend of Biko, and as a consequence was banned and had to escape the country with his family before, in London, he could write his book about Biko. In this book he describes meeting him for the first time in conditions of secrecy. Woods found him to be physically, a very big man, and angular in his attitude at first. Woods already knew him as the writer of many hard words against white society, including white Liberals who, it might have been thought, such a man as Biko might have regarded with some consideration. 'It will not be long' he had written in a student publication, 'before the blacks relate their poverty to their blackness in concrete terms. Because of the tradition forced onto the country, the poor people shall always be black people. It is not surprising, therefore, that they should wish to rid themselves of a system that locks up the wealth of the country in the hands of a few.'

But Woods soon discovered there was far more to Biko than anger, or bitterness over the condition of his own people. Woods wrote, after that first meeting, 'His quick brain, superb articulation of ideas and sheer mental force were highly impressive. He had the aura and stature of a leader. . . . Steve Biko, I later came to realize, was the greatest man I ever had the privilege to know.'

This greatness shone out, as was the testimony of many who knew him, from his whole character. He had, as Donald Woods says, charisma, personality and wisdom, together with integrity and courage. Had he lived, it seems that he would inevitably have become one of the black leaders which South Africa so desperately needs. It is a sad comment on the white treatment of the black over many generations in South Africa, that the latter tends to lack confidence in himself while in contact with whites. But it was certainly not the case with Biko, who showed complete poise, and had the power to transmit these qualities to those close to him. Like Wallenburg, he was not a Christian in the strict confessional sense; but Christian leaders spoke with great love of him. One was Father Stubbs, later Principal of the Federal Theological Seminary, who knew him when he was growing up, and who said that his great qualities were already becoming visible even at that early stage of his life. Another was Bishop Desmond Tutu, General Secretary of the South African Council of Churches, who spoke so movingly at Biko's funeral.

'When we heard the news "Steve Biko is dead"', he cried, 'we were struck dumb with disbelief. No, it can't be true! No, it must be a horrible nightmare, and we will awake and find that really it is different – that Steve is alive even if it be in detention. But no, dear friends, he is dead and we are still numb with grief, and groan with anguish "Oh God where are you? Oh God, do you really care – how can you let this happen to us?" It all seems such a senseless waste of a wonderfully gifted person, struck down in the bloom of youth, a youthful bloom that some wanted to see blighted. What could be the purpose of such wanton destruction? God, do you really love us? What must we do which we

136

have not done, what must we say which we have not said a thousand times over – that all we want is what belongs to all God's children, what belongs to an inalienable right – a place in the sun in our own beloved Mother Country. . . . How long can we go on appealing for a more just ordering of society where we all, black and white together, count not because of some accident of birth or a biological irrelevance – where all of us black and white count because we are human persons, human persons created in your own image.'

Such were the emotions which Steve Biko could arouse in good men. His funeral was most moving, as the press pictures of it testify. There was a coffin on an ox-cart, a straggling procession of black people following across the waste-land of a township. there his widow, very dignified, held Biko's little son, Samora. How could it be that a man of such qualities, with this power of attracting Christian admiration, could not himself be one with them in the faith? It is an exercise in Christian humility to ask the question.

Something of an answer emerged in an interview which Biko once gave to a Canadian who had come over from the Christian Institute for Christian Studies to interview prominent people, white and black, in the South African political scene. His talk with Biko, he wrote, was one of the most fruitful he had. It also is significant as about the last occasion when Biko was able at any length to speak of himself. In the course of this talk between the two, the Canadian asked him first what he meant by Black Consciousness. He was told that, for Biko, it meant the cultural and political revival of an oppressed people. Then, after he had developed this answer at length, he was asked how Christianity, in his view, related to this whole matter of black consciousness. His answer was a humbling one for the white Christian of the West. He grew up, he said, in the Anglican Church, it was important to him. But 'we as blacks cannot forget that Christianity in Africa is tied up with the entire colonial process. This meant that Christians came here with a form of culture which they called Christian but which in effect was Western, and which expressed itself as an Imperial culture as far as Africa was concerned. . . . It cannot be denied that in this situation many blacks, especially the young blacks, have begun to question Christianity. . . . black theology does not challenge Christianity itself but its Western package, in order to discover what the Christian faith means for our continent.' The lesson is challenging: Jesus does not distinguish between black or white, and must never be presented in terms which appear to tie it forever to the forms, customs, and ideas of one particular culture. Those who truly love the Lord just have to see this truth, or to continue to suffer the anguish of seeing such noble characters as Biko criticize them not for the faith they represent so much as for the package in which they wrap it. For the truth is always that 'there is neither Greek nor Jew, circumcision nor uncircumcision, Barbarian, Scythian, bond nor free; but Christ is all, and in all.' (Col. 3:11.)

The martyrdom of Biko began with arrest at a road block in the August of 1977. It reached its climax during his prolonged interrogation and torture in Security Police Headquarters in the Sanlam Building, Strand Street, Port Elizabeth. That he had been beaten into a coma, had sustained brain damage, and had died six days afterwards did not emerge into the world's news until almost a month later. When it did, the sensation and the sorrow was worldwide, except in South Africa itself. There was anger at the brutality involved and at the injustice which was so obvious. The inquest, held in the November of 1977 in Pretoria, revealed for the first time to many South Africans the ruthless nature of their Security Police. And though this inquest, closely followed by world media, revealed unmistakably the guilt of the police involved in what had been nothing less than murder, yet the final verdict was that 'on the available evidence death cannot be attributed to any act or omission amounting to a criminal offence on the part of any person.'

Significantly, Biko's family were nevertheless granted almost £35,000 as compensation. So, in relation to the martyrdom of Biko, those police directly involved, have to be accounted among the ranks who brought about other martyrdoms: the concentration camp guards who gassed Edith Stein in Auschwitz, the Japanese soldiery who slew Vivian Redlich, the SS who hanged Bonhoeffer, the Mau Mau who slew Kaguru, the men who shot Jonathan Daniels and Martin Luther King and, in another time and place, Archbishop Romero.

The reason why Steve Biko needs, for the love of God, to be included in the roll of those who have suffered as martyrs, can be found in his life, and was expressed with great clarity at that moving funeral. There were some 20,000 blacks present. There were several hundred whites, including Helen Suzman, a champion of the Black cause and for many years the only progressive party member of the South African Parliament, and representatives of all the major Christian Churches. But it was left to Bishop Tutu, in the closing words of his address, to make it clear why Biko, although he would not have claimed it, warrants a place among the Christian martyrs. Tutu said: 'Steve lived his life as one that was always being laid down for his friends and his enemies: so that his death, ghastly as it is, was a consummation of such a life – the greatest love a person can have for his friends is to lay down his life for them. Steve knew other words which that other remarkable young man, Jesus, had uttered: "In truth, in very truth, I tell you, a grain of wheat remains a solitary grain unless it falls into the ground and dies; but if it dies, it bears a rich harvest. The man who loves himself is lost, but he who hates himself in this world will be kept safe for eternal life. If anyone serves me, he must follow me; where I am, my servant will be. Whoever serves me will be honoured by my Father." (John 12.24:26).

So you see, Steve has started something that is quite unstoppable. The powers of evil, of injustice, of oppression, of exploitation, have done their worst, and have lost. They have lost because they are immoral and wrong, and our God, the God of Exodus, the liberator God, is a God of justice and righteousness, and he is on the side of justice and liberation and goodness. . . . We thank and praise God for giving us such a magnificent gift in Steve Biko, and for his sake, and the sake of ourselves and our children, let us dedicate ourselves anew to the struggle for the liberation of our beloved land, South Africa.'

This man, then, this Steve Biko, gave his life for his people. But it was a whole group, men and women together, who sacrificed themselves in what is now Zimbabwe one year later.

14
DEATH IN THE BUSH

Too numerous to be listed here individually by name — there were thirteen of them — those mission workers of the ELIM PENTECOSTAL CHURCH who died in Zimbabwe on a June night in 1978 are true members of the blessed company of martyrs, for they died, as they had lived, for their faith.

'I arrived at the scene three hours after the corpses were discovered', wrote a reporter in the Sunday Telegraph describing something which had happened in what was then Rhodesia in the June of 1978, 'Here on a grassy bank sheltered by acacia trees lay three family groups and their close friends. All had died an agonizing death.' He went on to describe how nearby there was a blackboard still bearing the score from the last game of cricket and, alongside, the body of an elderly woman with her hair in pink and white plastic curlers. A young woman in a blue jersey lay spread-eagled nearby, hand outstretched towards a three week-old baby. Elsewhere there were two other women, three small children, a man in a check shirt, a younger woman at a distance in long grass, living but unconscious. She died later. All had been killed with clubs and knives and most were unrecognizable. They all had been missionaries in the service of the Elim Pentecostal Church of the UK, working first in the Elim Mission in Katerere near the Mozambique border and later, in what was supposed to be a safer location, in what had once been a preparatory school for European boys/ in the picturesque Vumba Mountains, a once popular tourist area. This was the place where they met their deaths.

They were by no means the only Christian missionaries to

die in the course of what became known as 'the emergency' a civil war waged in the bush between Rhodesian Security Forces and the revolutionary Freedom Fighters seeking independence for what eventually emerged as the new nation of Zimbabwe. Neither their neutrality in this struggle, nor their manifest good intentions, nor their selfless service to the African people, spared these mission workers. Even before the June of 1978, when these nine Elim missionaries, together with four of their children, died, twenty others had been murdered. In the February of 1977, eight Roman Catholic mission workers, including four nuns, had been shot dead. Before that, in the December of 1976, a Roman Catholic Bishop, a priest and two nuns were held up as they were travelling by car and likewise killed, leaving only one survivor. A Swiss Roman Catholic priest, cycling on his way to preach at a church, vanished without trace. Later, a Minister of the Dutch Reformed Church, together with his wife, had died in an ambush. Another Roman Priest, last seen riding his motor cycle quite near the capital, Salisbury, was apparently abducted and murdered. Two other Catholic Missionaries, a German and a Swiss, met their deaths at a Mission School close to the Botswana border and two young Salvation Army women officers were gunned down when the Army Usher Institute was raided twenty miles from Bulawayo. All these had met martyr's deaths.

But there was something about the Elim tragedy which seemed to attract public attention, and to arouse pity, and a sense of shock, to an unusual degree. It could have been the numbers of those who perished at one and the same time – nine adults and four children. It could have been the methods of killing which seemed singularly brutal – knives and clubs. It could equally have been the close knit, family ties which bound these people together in a common cause, husbands and wives and friends. It could also have been that these were, to a striking degree ordinary people with, almost without exception, domestic backgrounds in a recognizable stratum of British society, largely provincial, almost entirely middle class. Not generally an environment productive of dramatic or heoric lives, it can seem all the more surprising when such lives do in fact emerge from it. Yet that was what happened in the case of these Elim Mission workers who perished on Saturday, 24 June 1978, on the campus of their school.

But, beyond all else, it would seem that the kind of faith these people professed was a considerable element contributing to the shock and pity aroused. Theirs was a faith based upon unquestioning trust in Christ as personal Lord and Saviour. These were people who gave their lives to him, without reservation. They would consult the Scriptures for guidance and seek his guidance in all their activities. They would be articulate in the use of such phrases as 'Giving one's life to Christ', 'Turning to him in prayer', 'Seeking the guidance of the Spirit', all hallowed phrases reflecting modes of faith common, it is true, to Christians; but used by these Elim Pentecostalists with particular conviction. None of them, or their successors, would lay claim to any uniqueness in these respects as regards other Christians who served with them in the mission field in Rhodesia. But the mixture of their particular kind of simple trust with the horrific deaths which came upon them undoubtedly made a very strong impression upon the public mind. So to unravel their story, and to see how they came to be where they were at that particular time which led so unexpectedly to their martyrs crowns, is to shed some further light upon the very nature of martyrdom itself. And to look a little into who and what these people were as persons is to make of their own martyrdoms all the more moving a story.

The Rhodesian Civil War had been going on a long time, building up as the years passed, especially following the declaration of Unilateral Independence, into an intensity of conflict which eventually came to involve the whole country. The pattern it developed was closely similar to that seen in other countries of the African Continent which, through varying degrees of bloodiness, have in the second half of this century achieved independence. The chief sufferers, as always, were those in the country areas – the bush. There, both white farmers and frightened and often terrorized African villagers, found themselves living at the sharp end of the conflict. For both 'the boys in the bush', the name by which the guerrillas became known, were an ever lurking terror. Roads were mined, farms raided, cattle killed, villagers intimidated, and their young people in some cases spirited away to join the insurgent forces over the border in Mozambique or elsewhere. The rival forces of Mugabe and N'Komo heavily armed and well organized, constituted formidable forces, and were engaged with a matching determination by those of the Government. The long continued fighting which developed was a heavy price to pay for the independence of Zimbabwe which eventually emerged. It was as is usual with guerrilla conflict, a hidden war of ambush, stealthy movements in the dark, mines under the roads, whispered threats and sudden deaths. To those missionaries of many churches who had come to this beautiful land to live among its often backward people, this war brought a severe test of constancy.

The Elim Pentecostal Church, a small Protestant denomination was, by comparison with some other Christian bodies in the field, relatively a newcomer. Its work in Rhodesia had started in 1946 through a sequence of events characteristic of the direct intervention and guidance of God which has always been a feature of the Pentecostal Movement. In that year a Doctor Cecil Brian and his wife, working in a mission hospital in Rhodesia, developed the conviction that it was God's will that they should go out into deep country where no missionaries had been before, and where there were no schools or hospitals and, most importantly, no knowledge of Jesus Christ, to work. Their conviction was strengthened by receiving a letter from another member of the Church back in England who told them how it had been revealed to him that it was God's will

144

that this should be so. It was followed by the discovery that there was a representative of their Church in Rhodesia already engaged in trying to discover where the opportunities of work lay. This man in his turn encountered a white Rhodesian who, he said, had had a dream in which he had seen five Africans coming towards him bearing empty pots, pleading for water. Furthermore, it seemed to him in his dream that he could identify them as being from the tribal area of a Chief Caterere, a poor and distant part of the country where the physical as well as the spiritual needs of the people were great. When, therefore, he met the man who had come out from England on behalf of the Elim Church to explore the possibilities of work, he mentioned this dream to him. The end result of this sequence of coincidences was that Doctor Brian and his wife were enabled to begin their work in a tent pitched by a stream from which base they preached and taught and lived the gospel. Twenty-five years later there was a one hundred bed hospital in Caterere, a school with 280 boarders, and a Church with numerous small Chapels scattered throughout the bush associated with it. All in all, Caterere represented a very considerable establishment, with something like 1000 people at any one time living around the Mission. It was some hundred miles north of Umtali, thirteen miles from the Mozambique border, and was placed at the foot of a steep hill in a valley.

This was not the place where the Elim Missionaries eventually met their martyrs deaths. That was in the Vumba after they had moved from Caterere. But this was the place to which all had felt moved to go and work. Among them was a quite elderly woman, Catherine Picken. She it was whose body was to be found with greying hair in pink and white plastic curlers. She had been, among other things, a games mistress, a netball adept, a first class hockey player in her youth and always a staunch and patient friend to all. She was not new to the mission field; but had served in the Congo and had had to make her escape from the Katanga Civil War. Maybe it was that experience which had made

145

her once wonder how she would herself face up to martyrdom. She had said: 'I don't know how I'd stand up to dying for Christ; but I am sure the Lord would give the grace for it if the time came.' As she was to discover, he did just that.

Then there was Mary Fisher, the only victim to be found still living at the scene of the massacre, and who died later. She was a gentle girl, with a striking soprano voice with which she would accompany herself on the guitar, to the delight of Africans who would gather around her and smile with her, and sing with her and sit all the more still to hear the preacher when Mary had prepared his way with a song. Wendy White, another of those later to die, had not been long with the Mission when it happened. A nurse, a teacher, a qualified social worker, she had much to give to God and to Africa and was ardently doing so up to the time of her death. So were Peter and Sandra McCann, he a Science Master at the Elim Secondary School at Caterere, she his devoted wife and mother of their baby girl, Joy.

In his own way had also Roy Lynn served the Lord. A Northern Irish man, with a family background of life on the land, he was also an expert maintenance man, skilled with machinery, happy offering his services to all. The African men teachers in particular liked to gather round him in his workshop and talk. He, during the time at Caterere, married the Hospital Matron, Joyce Pickering, a Yorkshire girl, a commonsense personality who made a splended counterweight to his sometimes disordered enthusiasms. She had delivered many babies in the hospital at Caterere, and it was therefore all the more a joy to everyone when she gave birth to one herself. This, Pamela, the child of Roy and Joyce, was three weeks old at the time of the massacre. She was battered to death and discovered lying just out of reach of her dead mother's outstretched arm.

Philip and Sue Evans, with their three children, made up another family in this tragic yet triumphant company of martyrs. They had married young, and both had come up the hard way. He had been a master in Nuneaton Secondary School, working at various times in a factory and on a farm, and had acquired two higher degrees. Sue, his wife, had supported him in all his years of study, taking on extra work in order to do so. These two, as she herself put it in a letter 'had made our lives available to God, and he wants to use them now.' For both of them, acceptance of the challenge to go and work in Africa was a daunting one, representing a huge change from urban life in the English Midlands. These, then, were some of those destined to achieve the crown of martyrdom.

None of them, however, had felt really threatened by the activities of the Patriotic Front or Freedom Fighters 'the Boys in the Bush'. It was not until a certain night in the April of 1976 that the threat which these people represented became a reality. On that night the Evans, Sue and Philip, had staying with them Joan Caudell, also on the School staff of the Elim Secondary School at Caterere. The place was unusually quiet, several other members of the staff, including the Principal, Peter Griffiths, being away. But there had been rumours of an incident at a Catholic Mission not far away where a group of the terrorists had gone by night and spoken in a threatening manner. In this atmosphere Miss Caudell accepted the invitation of Sue Evans to stay the night with them. The three, after listening to the radio, prayed together and then prepared for bed.

Then came a banging on their door. When Phil Evans went into the hallway he could see, through the mesh screen, the faces of three men in battledress. With them was one of the African teachers of the School who said, in a frightened manner, that these visitors wanted to talk. Phil did not open the door, but one of the men addressed him through the window, saying they were Freedom Fighters, that they had come to liberate the African people. Sue Evans, who was standing behind her husband, could hear all that was said. She heard Phil say that they were Missionaries; that they were not involved in politics 'We don't preach politics in

147

this mission', he said, 'we preach Jesus Christ and his love for us all – black and white. He died for us all, then rose again, and he is alive today. That's what we preach here.' There followed a memorable rejoinder from one of the men who appeared to be the leader of the group. He said: 'I used to believe what you believe. I was a Methodist Preacher once. I prayed that God would liberate us Africans, but he didn't answer. So now I trust in this!' And he indicated his gun.

After some time, during which this same leader made a further political speech, they asked for medicines and food. These handed out, they left, warning the Evans that if they contacted the Security Forces, they would come back and kill them. When the men had gone, the three missionaries knelt in prayer, the children still sleeping quietly in an adjoining room.

Another member of the Staff who was disturbed that night was Sister Joy Bath. First, her dog barking woke her. Then, when she had got out of bed and went outside, intending to bring the animal in to quieten him, in case his noise disturbed her parents, who happened to be staying with her, she saw a man standing. He was one of the African teachers in the School. He told her that 'some visitors' had come to see her. It was, of course, the same group who had visited the Evans'. They proclaimed themselves loudly and together as Freedom Fighters, and their leader made the same political speech as he had done at the other house. Among them, as she grew used to the darkness, Sister Bath saw the figure of Joyce Pickering, her nursing colleague, who had been brought from her house by the group. They asked, as before, for drugs and, reluctantly, the two women supplied them from the hospital's stores. And with that they went.

Meanwhile, Mr and Mrs Bath, staying with their daughter, had heard the disturbance. Both of them rose from their beds and, standing hand in hand, prayed while the voices were speaking outside in the night. When the two nurses, their own daughter, and Joyce Pickering, went in to them they were still murmuring these prayers. When the four of them were together, and the light was on, Mr Bath proposed a reading from the Bible. His copy had a subject index, and in this he looked up the word 'fear'. And then he read to them from Psalm 91: 'He who dwells in the shelter of the most high, who abides in the shadow of the Almighty, will say to the Lord, "My refuge and my fortress; my God, in whom I trust".' He ended at verse 5: 'You will not fear the error of the night.'

As the months went by tension in the whole country increased as what was now quite clearly a general war intensified. The sound of exploding landmines was heard frequently out at Caterere; on some occasions casualties from such incidents were brought into the mission hospital, and it became necessary to travel around in vehicles especially strengthened against this weapon. But it was only after much heart searching and prayer that the decision was eventually taken by the Elim Authorities to move the mission back away from the border to what was hopefully considered a safer area. Thirteen miles from the town of Umtali, were the buildings of what had been the Eagle Preparatory School for European boys. The Emergency, as the war was called, had emptied it. The move there was a big undertaking; the number of pupils the mission had to accommodate was, for one thing, far larger than that which the original school had provided for. The accommodation, too, was of a different nature and the region, although beautiful, lacked the familiarity of Caterere. But eventually the change was accomplished and the work of this Elim Secondary School assured, it was hoped, for some time to come.

But, so far as this group of teachers was concerned, that was not to be. Political and military conditions worsened: areas nearer the town became as vulnerable to violence as once had been those nearer the borders. Although their new location in the Vumba was near Umtali, the time came when authorities recommended that the white teachers of the Elim

School should find themselves accommodation in the town and sleep there, going out to the school to teach only by day. After all, the Roman Catholic School on the Botswana border had closed; so had the Salvation Army Usher Institute after its tragedy. So they all made their own individual arrangements and soon were ready for this further move. It remained only to pack up their belongings and move into the town. But they were not to reach that stage. Instead, a momentous fate awaited them. The nature of that fate was perhaps indicated by some words in the reading from *Daily Light* which the missionary Catherine Picken found in her evening reading just before what was to have been her move, with that of others, into Umtali. 'Beloved, think it not strange concerning the fiery trial which is to try you.'

Thus it befell that, on the night of 23 June 1978, they were all preparing to pack up and move house into Umtali. Some of them regretted the move from Caterere; but all recognized its necessity and were prepared to adapt themselves, with their customary self dedication, to the new arrangements. The situation was not easy; there were murmurs among some African employees and even some pupils. Phil Evans, who by this time was acting as Principal, felt the stress of this particularly. But he, together with all his colleagues, as dedicated people, were prepared to face whatever should befall.

It was a quiet evening. The houses of the various missionaries stood up on the hillside, somewhat isolated from the school and, with their lights on, easily picked out by anyone approaching through the bush. And there were those approaching – a band of men moving stealthily towards them. In these houses, the scenes were domestic and familiar. Joyce Pickering, the hospital Matron who had married the Northern Irishman, Roy Lynn, was at home with her husband and three week old baby. The McCanns had just finished their supper; Catherine Picken, who was so good on the games field, was marking examination papers.

150

Philip and Sue Evans were still at supper. Mary and Wendy, the two girls, were nearby in their flats. One of them was writing a letter which ended, 'with much love in Jesus, Wendy'. It was this girl who was to die in hospital in Salisbury a week later, the only one of the party to survive, even if briefly, the actual killings.

They were taken, all of them, with the four children, out into the bush and slain. It was revealed at the inquest that the troop of guerrillas had rounded up the African pupils and staff of the school and commanded them to stay in until dawn. One of them had been taken out in order to open up the school office and he testified at the inquest that he had seen Phil Evans with his hands tied behind his back. The only direct evidence as to what happened from that point was an entry in a notebook found on the body of one of the raiding party who, weeks after the killings at the school, had himself been shot by the Security Forces. The entry read: 'On Friday, 23 June 1978 is the day and date we reached Ngue Mission on Vumba area near Matondo Camp in Zimunya District. Time of operation from 6.30 to 9.00 p.m. . . . Total number of comrades who were there 21. . . . Weapons used, axes and knobkerries. Aim: to destroy the enemies. We killed 12 whites, including four babies . . .'.

A great impact was made by the tragedy upon the general mind. The killings were reported world-wide. The funeral Service held in Umtali had a congregation of 800 Europeans and Africans. None of the relatives, who had been flown out to attend at the expense of the Elim Church, expressed any bitterness, only forgiveness.

'The world will see that killing one Christian is actually multiplying us', wrote an African who had been a pupil in the school. 'The blood of the Church martyrs is the seed for new Christians. In this way the Church will triumph when it is oppressed and progress when it is despised. Now I believe that it is my duty to spread the Gospel.'

The Universal Church has always loved to dwell upon the role of its martyrs, and to see them in the minds eye as a glorious company with an honoured position in Heaven itself. Therefore it is good to think of these humble men and women of the Elim Church mingling there with Edith Stein, who died in Auschwitz, with Dietrich Bonhoeffer, with Martin Luther King, with Janani Luwum, Archbishop of Uganda, with Oscar Romero, Archbishop in Salvador whose martyrdom was the most recent of those recorded in this book.

15

CHAMPION OF THE POOR

OSCAR ROMERO, Archbishop of San Salvador, was originally a conforming churchman who, moved by the call for justice for his oppressed people, became their champion and died for it, seeing in their needs the demands of Christ to serve them.

The date was 24 March 1980. The place was the Chapel of The Divine Providence in San Salvador. The occasion was a Memorial Mass being celebrated by a small, gentle man, Oscar Arnulfo Romero, Archbishop of San Salvador. He was saying this Mass for the mother of a journalist friend. As he reached the words of the Consecration: 'This is my body given for you . . . this is my blood shed for you . . .' a shot rang out and the Archbishop fell to the ground, killed instantly by a bullet through the heart.

His was one of many martyrdoms which took place, and which are still taking place, in that country in Central America. Its population of just five million is bitterly poor and largely illiterate, at the same time held down by a military dictatorship maintained and supported by fourteen land owning ruling families. Fifty years ago an attempt to improve the conditions of the people was put down by force, and this force has been maintained ever since. Meanwhile, the oppression of the people has increased and their poverty has become more severe. Thirty thousand people died in the insurrection of the early 1930s; many thousands have died in the 1970s and '80s as opposition groups have emerged, drawn from many different sources – peasants, students, factory workers – but all devoted to the same cause: the relief of the intolerable conditions of the poor. The whole situation has been greatly aggravated by international tensions. The United States, with its fear of Communist influence in Central America and its apprehension of possible Soviet backed infiltrations from Cuba has seemed at times to back the military dictatorship although, increasingly, American public opinion has been turning away from this stance. It is a tragic situation for a poverty stricken people caught and crushed in a collision of great forces.

In the centre stands the Roman Catholic Church. But this itself has been going through a period of dramatic change. On the one hand stands the institutional Church which has tended to support the power structures of society. On the other, down in the grass roots, there have been, and are, liberationist movements concerned to see that the Church identifies wholly with the poor and the oppressed. What is happening in El Salvador reflects what is happening elsewhere in Latin America – the rediscovery by the Church of a new role as the servant of the people rather than of the power structures which have ruled them hitherto. Such a development, associated with what has been called 'liberation theology', is wide open to the suspicion that it represents an infiltration of a Communist ideology into the very body of the Church itself. There are those who see dangers in this situation. It is the age-long difficulty involved in Christ's command 'Render unto Caesar the things that are Caesar's, and unto God the things that are God's.' Which is which? Where is the line between them to be drawn?

But such theoretical questions are never likely to reach the oppressed people of El Salvador. However they have certainly infiltrated the Church there, so that, among much else, there has arisen a new generation of politically conscious priests.

So there have been martyrs in El Salvador: many cases in which people have, in the classic pattern throughout the

154

ages, suffered for the faith. There was Father Rafael Palacios, a popular Pastor murdered in 1979; there was the priest Alirio Napoleon Macias, struck down at his own altar later in the same year; there was the Jesuit, Rutilioe Grande, who met his death in 1977, and Alfonso Navarro assassinated in the same year. Since Romero's death the murdering has gone on. In 1980 four American women missionaries, Maura Clarke, Ita Ford, Jean Donovan and Dorothy Kazel were slain together in the December of 1980 and their bodies left by the roadside. There is a long and tragic list of such martyrs, and this violence has been accompanied by acts of sacrilege: churches destroyed by bands of troops, altars overthrown and the Communion bread scattered upon the ground.

Romero himself has emerged as a hero of the people, and it is as such that his memory will survive. The inspiration of his story lies in the manner in which this fundamentally gentle and timid man reacted to the challenges of the situation in which he found himself and, in so reacting, developed the courage of a martyr. A product of the Institutional Church, he came to recognize the truth that he could not be faithful to Christ without moving into opposition and taking the side of the oppressed. This was the heart of the matter, and because it is so important an issue for Christians in any age, it is important to try to trace the path which led him eventually to that assassin's bullet as he stood by the altar in the Chapel of The Divine Providence Cancer Hospital in San Salvador. His martyrdom was a result of the situation in which he found himself, something which is almost universally true of martyrs throughout the ages. It would have been much simpler, and certainly much easier for him, if he had chosen to go along with the situation and to act as a conforming prelate. But God had other plans for him.

Romero was born of working class parents in 1917. Ordained in 1942, he went to the Gregorian University in Rome in the following year. After a time as a Parish Priest he became Secretary to a Bishop, Rector of the Cathedral, Director of the Seminary in San Miguel and 1966 Secretary General of the Bishops Conference of El Salvador. By 1970 he was an auxilliary Bishop, four years later a Bishop, and in 1977 Archbishop of San Salvador.

His own priests at first did not think highly of him. The view of him expressed at a meeting of priests involved in the Underground Movement, when it first became known that he was to be Archbishop, was unenthusiastic. He was said to be quiet – certainly a man of prayer. Socially and politically, his outlook was, it was said, very conventional. There seemed little grounds for hope that in the new Archbishop a dynamic leader was to be found.

Savage oppression was demonstrated in the early days of Romero's archiepiscopate. His very installation was taken as an opportunity by the authorities to step up their reign of terror against the Church. Priests were tortured and murdered. There also took place at this time a massacre when many thousands had gathered together for a meeting concerned with the peoples' struggle. Most of the liberationist parties were represented, and the meeting was concerned with the fraudulent proceedings which had characterized a recent election. But the gathering, surrounded by the National Guard, was fired upon. Many took refuge in a church; many were killed on its steps and those who managed to get in were caught by the gas which the military threw into them. A message which was distributed among the crowd on that occasion from a political activist said: 'The Church is where it always should have been; with the people, surrounded by wolves.' Romero, after this event, when faced with the facts of it, indicated, to the surprise of many, that he agreed. The fundamental change in this once conforming and conventional priest had begun.

The pace of change now quickened. The martyrdom of Rutilio Grande on 12 March 1977 accelerated it. Grande, a Jesuit Priest, had been totally identified with the cause of the Campesinos, the peasant poor of the countryside. Romero, by this time Archbishop, went to the scene and saw the blood-stained body of the shot priest, together with two of his friends, lying on the floor of the church, surrounded by poor people singing revolutionary songs. Romero was deeply moved. It was a deed which caused fundamental changes in Romero's thinking.

He abandoned, in the first place, any idea of keeping henceforth, as a conforming churchman, on the side of the Law. If the Law was evil, as it clearly was, then it was there to be broken. Thus when, about this time, public meetings were forbidden, he called for public demonstrations. He also put an embargo on further dialogue with the Government until some of its manifest injustices, including the murder of Rutilio, had been explained. He encouraged the development of new liturgies, novel and more meaningful modes of expressing the Church's worship in a revolutionary situation which were widely seen as means whereby the Church could express its own response to the contemporary challenge. He was fiercely criticized for this, as for many other innovations that he brought in at this time. One of them was an encouragement, on a greater scale than had been known before, of Church unity. Yet another was the call to a new kind of devotion to the needs of the people, so that the Church could become the voice of those who had no voice. It was not easy to bring these changes to pass. The mass celebrations of the Eucharist, often a feature of these changes, were regarded as dangerous gatherings by many, and as unholy disorders by others. The pressure on Romero from his critics became severe.

But the price was heavy. The martyrdoms continued, and what happened at a place called Aguilares was only too sadly typical of what was taking place elsewhere. The peasants had tried to take some land in order to grow a crop. Soldiers moved in; all the houses were searched. If a bible was found the owners were either beaten or killed. Four American Jesuit Priests were beaten, taken to the Guatemalan border and expelled, while a Salvadorian Priest was handcuffed taken to gaol and tortured. In the church itself the Communion breads were thrown to the floor, as on other occasions elsewhere, and 300 villagers were held in gaol while the whole village was occupied for a month. When this was reported to Romero he was deeply distressed, and urged shelter and succour for fugitives.

He was now learning fast about the real conditions of the people. When, on one occasion, he visited a remote village he was at first hurt not to be given any meal. It was only later he realized the people simply had no food. But he was also beginning to make an impact on the Salvadorian national scene. His broadcast sermon on a Sunday began to attract a very large audience indeed. It became dangerous to listen to him, so that the sale of earphones rose sharply as it became risky to have that voice coming loud over a car radio or into a house.

By this time he was making an impact also on the international scene, and was nominated for the Nobel Peace Prize. Speaking at the University of Louvain, in Belgium, in the February of 1980 he made unmistakably clear what his position had by that time become. 'I am a shepherd who, with his people, has begun to learn a beautiful and difficult truth: our Christian faith requires that we submerge ourselves in this world. The course taken by the Church has always had political repercussions. The problem is how to direct that influènce so that it will be in accordance with the faith. The world that the Church must serve is the world of the poor, and the poor are the ones that decide what it means for the Church to live really in the world.'

And again; 'The Church has committed itself to the world of the poor. . . . The words of the prophets of Israel still hold true for us. There are those who would sell the just man for money, and a poor man for a pair of sandals. There are those who fill their houses with violence, fill their houses with what they have stolen. There are those who crush the poor, while lying on beds of the most exquisite marble. There are those who take over house after house, field after field, until

158

they own the whole territory and are the only ones in it.'

The voice of Amos coming down the centuries is unmistakable: 'Woe to those who lie upon beds of ivory, and stretch themselves upon their couches . . . hear this, you who trample upon the needy, and bring the poor of the land to an end, saying, "When will the new moon be over, that we may sell grain? And the Sabbath, that we may offer wheat for sale . . . that we may buy the poor for silver and the needy for a pair of sandals. . . ."' (Amos 6:4 and 8:4–6.)

It is perfectly clear that he knew, before it came, what his end was to be. Writing in a Mexican paper within two months of his death, he said: 'My life has been threatened many times. I have to confess that, as a Christian, I don't believe in death without resurrection. If they kill me, I will rise again in the Salvadoran people. . . . As a shepherd I am obliged by Divine Law to give my life for those I love, for the entire Salvadoran people, including those who threaten to assassinate me. If they should go so far as to carry out their threats, I want you to know that I now offer my blood to God for justice and the resurrection of El Salvador. Martyrdom is a grace of God that I do not feel worthy of. But if God accepts the sacrifice of my life, my hope is that my blood will be like a seed of liberty and a sign that our hopes will soon become a reality.'

When the shot eventually came which killed him it was clear why it had been fired. As a friend of the people he had become an enemy of their rulers. Bishops who gathered at Romero's funeral were quite clear about this and said as much in a statement issued at the time: 'For defending the lives of his people and striving for a society of justice and peace, he was murdered, like Christ, at the moment of offertory. We have come here representing our churches and our peoples, to protest this horrendous crime, and to celebrate with the Salvadoran people and Church the new life that his martyrdom will invigorate.'

Whether in fact it has achieved that end is as yet by no means clear. Martyrdoms, in this world, do not generally have happy endings. El Salvador is still a strife torn society: it is still subject to internal repression and external tension. But a splendid thing has emerged, nonetheless, from the martyrdom of Oscar Arnulfo Romero, the conventional churchman who became a Christian activist deeply involved with movements for the liberation of the people. That splendid thing has been his resurrection, because he still lives in the hearts and minds of his people and because also, it is to be hoped, he still lives as a challenge to the consciences of many Christians throughout the world who have not been called upon to face so severe a challenge. As one who was present at his funeral said: 'His resurrection is not a future event. It is a present reality. He is life for us now, and that is why we must defeat the forces of death in El Salvador and wherever Jesus continues to be crucified.'

Select Bibliography

Daily Life in the Early Church by G. G. Davies (Lutterworth)

The Desert My Dwelling Place by Elisabeth Hamilton (Hodder & Stoughton)

Saints of the Twentieth Century by Br Kenneth (Mowbray)

China and the Cross by Columba Carey Elwes (Longmans)

Commandant of Auschwitz by Rudolph Hoess (Pan Books)

Scholar and the Cross: the life and work of Edith Stein by H. C. Graeff (Longmans)

Righteous Gentile by John Bierman (Allen Lane)

Dietrich Bonhoeffer by Mary Bosanquet (Hodder & Stoughton)

So Rough a Wind by Sir Michael Blundell (Weidenfeld & Nicholson)

The Martyrs by Jack Mendelsohn (Harper & Row Inc., NY)

Martin Luther King, A Critical Biography by David L. Lewis (Allen Lane)

Janani by Margaret Ford (Marshall, Morgan & Scott)

Biko by Donald Woods (Paddington Press)

The Voice of One Crying in the Wilderness by Bishop Desmond Tutu (Mowbray)

The Rainbow and the Thunder by Phyllis Thompson (Hodder & Stoughton)

Romero, Martyr of Salvador (Lutterworth Press)